TINY HOMES

Effective Tips and Techniques for Designing, Building and Living in Tiny Homes

ANDREW BERGER

© Copyright 2020 - All rights reserved.

The content contained within this book may not be reproduced, duplicated, or transmitted without direct written permission from the author or the publisher.

Under no circumstances will any blame or legal responsibility be held against the publisher, or author, for any damages, reparation, or monetary loss due to the information contained within this book, either directly or indirectly.

Legal Notice:

This book is copyright protected. It is only for personal use. You cannot amend, distribute, sell, use, quote or paraphrase any part, or the content within this book, without the consent of the author or publisher.

Disclaimer Notice:

Please note the information contained within this document is for educational and entertainment purposes only. All effort has been executed to present accurate, up to date, reliable, complete information. No warranties of any kind are declared or implied. Readers acknowledge that the author is not engaging in the rendering of legal, financial, medical, or professional advice. The content within this book has been derived from various sources. Please consult a licensed professional before attempting any techniques outlined in this book.

By reading this document, the reader agrees that under no circumstances is the author responsible for any losses, direct or indirect, that are incurred as a result of the use of the information contained within this document, including, but not limited to, errors, omissions, or inaccuracies.

Table of Contents

Introduction 1

Chapter 1: What Makes A Tiny Home? **6**

What Is A Tiny Home? 6

Common Obstacles and Solutions.................................... 8

Common Misconceptions.. 16

Chapter 2: Why Live In A Tiny Home?....................................**21**

Pros of Living in a Tiny Home 21

Cons of Living in a Tiny Home....................................... 28

Chapter 3: Design - What You Need to Know? **33**

So, What Are My Options? 34

Chapter 4: Building-What Materials Will I Need?.....................**54**

Additional Options... 63

Chapter 5: Finishing Up-Things to Pay Attention To **69**

Chapter 6: Living in a Tiny Home **80**

Chapter 7: Tips and Tricks **100**

Conclusion **108**

iv

Introduction

A tiny home is exactly what it says on the tin, a house that is much smaller than one might usually imagine. Can you imagine living in a space that's around 150-400 square feet? Well, it's easier than you think!

Imagine living your life far away from the ideas of rent, mortgaging, and possibly even bills. Some tiny homes have the ability to make their own electricity, and capture their own water! Today, you'll find that most people go into some amount of debt due to housing. With a tiny home, you can almost eliminate any need for debt (there have been cases of tiny houses being built for as little as $500!)

Because of the current economic climate, together with the rapid progression of global warming, many have elected to rethink the way they live. This is part of the roots of the tiny house movement. It's especially popular in the USA, where a lot of people have faced homelessness, and renting is an ever-present issue.

Now, you might think that the tiny home movement demands a great sacrifice, but you couldn't be more wrong! Owning a tiny home isn't about sacrificing anything; it's about living a bigger life in a smaller house.

A tiny house brings much more simplicity. How many times have you looked at an old piece of furniture or something you've scarcely ever used and thought, "Why is that even still here?" Well, if you live in a tiny home, you won't ever have this thought again!

Living in a tiny home comes with massive advantages when it comes to finances. Rent in a big city can easily go for a couple of thousand dollars a month. Imagine if instead, you could put this money into your retirement savings, or if you could invest it.

Okay, let's assume you don't have any problems with money. Let's even go as far as to say you've amassed a fortune. Would you still have a reason to move into a tiny home? Are tiny homes simply a way to lower expenses?

Living in a tiny home means that you are using a lot less space, making it with fewer materials than a regular house, and are using less energy for utilities. This, in turn, means that your carbon footprint quickly plummets. This is extremely important today when global warming is an ever-looming threat. The tiny house trend is making the world a better place for everyone!

But even if climate change weren't a thing, there would still be ample reason to live in one. For example, simplicity- our lives in the 21st century are constantly cluttered, complicated, and are becoming increasingly more difficult to navigate around. In this complexity, a tiny home lets you retreat to a smaller, simpler space and makes us rethink everything we consume.

Now, you might think that a house this small would be too small to house everything that you need, but you'd be wrong. Almost all tiny homes have enough room to fit in a small living area, sleeping loft, kitchen, and bathroom. All of this in so little space that a trailer could move it!

This is another benefit of tiny homes. While some tiny homes are built upon a solid foundation, others aren't and are mobile enough to move around with a truck or even a car. This means that you no longer need to own the very land your house sits on. It's even possible for a tiny home to be wholly self-contained. This means that you get your water from rain or through filtering river water and that you get your electricity off the grid.

Let's make a comparison.

In the US, a standard house is about \$270 000 to buy at once, or \$481 000, at an interest rate of 4.25% over a period of 30 years. Now, your average tiny home will only set you back \$23 000. This is over ten times cheaper. If you compare it to the latter figure, the difference becomes over 20 times.

The difference between owning a standard house and a tiny home is approximately \$257, 000.

The data supports this. Tiny home owners tend to have a lot more saved up than people that own standard-size housing. They also tend to earn more, as well as be in far less debt.

A tiny house also means fewer bills. Most of the time, you'll be spending the vast majority of say, your electricity bill, on heating. Meanwhile, a tiny house will have much less space to heat, lowering the bill even if you choose to stick to the grid.

Now, this is not to say that living in a tiny home has no downsides, it does. For example, most people will have their sleeping lofts be close to the ceiling. Because hot air goes up rather than down, you'll most likely have to install a fan to lower the temperature inside.

On the other hand, this also means you'll be having a much easier time sleeping in winter when temperatures drop lower. There's also societal pressure and other issues that many tiny home owners face.

So, with that established, let's go through what we'll be covering in this book.

First, we'll be going over everything that goes into a tiny home. In the 1st chapter, we'll cover a little bit of everything so you can get acquainted with all of the elements of making and owning a tiny home.

Next, we'll look over the "why" of living in a tiny home. While we touched upon it in this section, we'll be expanding upon most of our arguments.

In the 3rd chapter, we'll be talking about design. The design of a home is one of its most important elements, and as such, we'll go over the most important things you need to know about designing your own home.

You can skip the 4th chapter if you're planning to buy a tiny home. It is dedicated to those who have decided that they want to build their own, rather than having a firm do it for them. We'll go over the materials that you need to procure to make a tiny home.

In the 5th chapter, we'll mention some of the most common pitfalls of living and building a tiny home, as well as how to avoid them.

The 6th chapter covers living in a tiny home. Despite the numerous advantages of doing so, living in a tiny home can be hard to adjust to for many of us, and I know it was for me because it simply isn't what we're used to. To help alleviate this, we'll be talking about the most common challenges and tips for living in a tiny home.

The 7th chapter covers tips and tricks, things that don't quite fit into the rest of the chapters but are still useful for you to know.

So, let's dive into the expansive world of tiny homes. I think you'll be surprised at what a fun and exciting journey it can be!

Chapter 1

What Makes A Tiny Home?

In this chapter, we'll be going over what a tiny home is, and some of their common properties. This is designed to help you understand what is involved in designing and building a tiny home and living the tiny-home life.

We'll also be going over some initial challenges that tiny home owners are faced with when they're making their home.

What Is A Tiny Home?

Put simply, a tiny home is just a home that's not very large in area. What separates a tiny home from, say, a shed is that the tiny home operates as a whole house. To call something a tiny home, it needs to have all of the necessary facilities to conduct everyday life.

Now, while some extreme tiny homes might only have a bathroom, and a combined sleeping and kitchen area, this is by no means the norm. A regular tiny home has every element of a regular home, just downsized.

Something tiny homes are famous for is their clever use of space. You'll find that building and living in a tiny home in grains within you a new appreciation for empty spaces. For example, you might have your "living-room" on the lowest floor, right next to the stairs that bring you to your sleeping area. The lack of hallways between rooms means that you're able to get from one room to another much quicker.

These elements make some aspects of living much easier. For example, you're highly unlikely to leave your stove on if you can see it from your living room.

With that being said, there are also some downsides that come with living in such a small space. For example, you won't be able to keep your motorcycle indoors. The lack of space can sometimes present an issue; however, clever design and object placement can make up for pretty much all of these issues.

A tiny home is also often associated with being very green and eco-friendly. Utilizing rainwater is quite common among owners of tiny homes. Furthermore, when you build a tiny home, there is much less waste than you get with a standard-sized house. They also use up a lot fewer resources compared to regular houses.

Owning a tiny home is also associated with being self-sufficient. Tiny homes tend to have their own electricity generators, and some even grow their own food!

Common Obstacles and Solutions

Owning a tiny home isn't easy. There's a number of challenges that come with living in a tiny home. Fortunately, they also have solutions. If you're feeling conflicted about your tiny home for any of these reasons, know you aren't alone, and that it'll be worth it in the end.

Getting Access to Land

A prime issue that any homeowner faces is access to land. If you don't have land to build upon, well, you'll have a rough time. This is one of the biggest barriers to entry of living in a tiny home. The land is getting increasingly more expensive as more people are populating the planet. If you want to balance the area being close to your job in addition to being affordable, your search for the right land may be harder. Now, thankfully a tiny home doesn't take too much space. With that being said, it's ideal for placing your house a bit away from the prying eye, as curmudgeons can be quite an eyesore.

Now, the solution to this issue, unfortunately, isn't very simple. The land will always be pricy no matter what you do. With that being said, there are a few corners you might be able to cut to bring it to a more affordable price. The first and foremost is to look at more rural areas. If you're able to work from home, then living in a rural area connected to the city by public transport shouldn't be too much issue.

You can also look at the land that has failed the perc test. A perc, or percolation test is a test that checks the water absorption rate of the nearby soil. In this case, you'll need to figure out how to gain access to water and waste disposal, but it will bring down the price significantly.

Another solution is to simply park your tiny house behind someone's regular house or in their yard. You'll be surprised at how many people are willing to give you part of their land in exchange for a meager sum of money. Sometimes, you might find they're even willing to do this for free.

Another option is co-housing or cooperative purchasing, this is where you find a set of people that also want to buy land, and you all buy it together. This is a pretty decent option in case you don't mind having a few neighbors.

Issues Getting Loans

Now, while many tiny home owners make them without ever getting in debt for a dime, this can't always be expected. Some people simply don't have the money to spare. In these situations, you might encounter issues with banks. This is due to the fact that tiny homes are generally not very valuable when it comes to resale.

With this comes the fact that most banks will feel that they aren't worth much as collateral.

Solving this one is quite difficult. In general, banks aren't fond of taking risks, which makes taking out a loan for a tiny home difficult. On the other hand, taking out a personal loan might work. This is due to the fact that tiny homes simply don't take too much money to build.

Another option is to save up. While it's understandable to want to have your home immediately, sometimes the right call is to wait. This is probably the way I'd recommend the most. Part of the appeal of tiny homes is getting into one without racking up any debt.

You can also settle for lower-quality (or simply throwaway) materials. You'll find that people commonly throw away perfectly fine building materials. If you're fine with taking a bit of time and effort to build it, you can build a perfectly serviceable tiny home out of materials people threw into the bin. Furthermore, people often give away free furniture on sites such as Craigslist, which can help you equip your home quickly.

Now, it's also possible to use a low APR credit card to pay for the tiny home, and then treat the bills as if they were your loan payments. Personally, I wouldn't advise this approach, as it carries a lot more risk than it's worth.

Some Places Have Laws against Them

Now, while some people will swear up and down that simply attaching your tiny house to a trailer is enough to make it immune to legislation. Unfortunately, this isn't the case in many places. In some places, there's a minimum habitable structure definition, which will often exclude tiny houses.

You need to research the laws of where you're intending to live prior to building your tiny house. Otherwise, you risk building the house only to get into problems with law enforcement immediately after. In many places in the US, code enforcement will come after tiny home owners quite often.

Laws are potentially the hardest of these issues to solve. The first step to doing so is for you to make a decision: are you going to adhere to the law to a T, or are you willing to cut corners a little? Note that not abiding the law does have very real consequences.

The easiest way to get legal recognition for your tiny home is to have the professionals handle it. There's a variety of companies you'll read about later that will handle the legislation for you. Note that this will be more expensive, but it can easily be worth it when compared to breaking the law.

An alternative is to pay a contractor or developer separately to have them help you get around codes and the whole permitting process. Learning how to do all of this on your own is a time-consuming endeavor, and likely won't be worth it. Always do your research before going to any professionals. Have drawings, plans, and codes of other tiny houses at the ready.

Now, if you're planning to skirt around the law, that has its own consequences too. While it isn't very common for tiny home owners to get into trouble with the law, it is technically possible for them to charge you in many places.

The first thing you'll want to do is find out the exact wording of the law. Ensure that you're following it to the best of your ability, and recognize that you might face the consequences regardless. If you're going to be breaking the law, make sure you're at least legal savvy enough to talk to code enforcement professionally. This will take quite a bit of time, but if you ever encounter any issues, it'll be a godsend. Furthermore, your country might have lost enough laws for you to get away on a technicality. If all else fails, remember that in most cases, you're trying to show nobody lives in the tiny house, and you're living elsewhere.

To lessen the chances of getting into trouble, you should ensure that you're the kind of person that won't be reported to law enforcement. In other words, be a good neighbor. Most investigations start from a complaint, rather than a spontaneous investigation. Furthermore, it might make you a couple of friends!

The Intense Social Pressures We Face

Today's society is all about going bigger. A bigger monitor, a bigger phone, a bigger car, a bigger home. The norms are all tilted towards the idea that more and bigger is better. Living in a tiny house goes contrary to today's societal norms. This can make some people act quite irrationally towards tiny house owners. For example, they might make fun of it, or they might criticize your decision relentlessly for no apparent reason. Since people work every day to acquire as many things as they can, even implying that you do not want to do that sounds like you're saying they're living life wrong. This can end up in people getting defensive.

First and foremost, make sure you don't sound like a preacher when talking about your lifestyle. It's incredibly critical that you sound like a person making a choice, rather than sounding like you consider yourself superior to everyone else. Keep in mind that everyone else is also making their choice, and they're just as valid as yours.

Organizations like Treehugger have tackled the issue of societal pressure head-on. Lloyd Alter has pointed out that much of the world is currently living in small houses. He then questioned where the Western world's obsession with bigger houses comes from. Now, note that the societal pressures we're discussing here aren't global trends, but rather day to day interactions with the local people.

There's no right way to deal with societal pressure. It's a problem that all people face at some point in their lives. However, I believe that having a good understanding of oneself, as well as being confident in your choices is the first step. In case you do get into an argument, try to present your point with a respectful tone.

Fear of the Unknown

Let's face it, putting tens of thousands of dollars on a project is never easy. This is especially true when it's something that goes so far against social norms, and represents a huge change to one's lifestyle. Living in a tiny home isn't all sunshine and rainbows; it can be quite a scary prospect. This is especially true, the closer you get to the moment where you have to decide whether or not to go for it, where you have to make that final leap of faith and go for it.

This is where fear and self-doubt rear their heads. You'll be mulling over whether or not the doubts you're having are just a normal reaction to a huge change, or if they are your subconscious to tell you aren't ready. Sorting through these negative thoughts can easily take a toll on you, and even the people that are used to change will feel a bit lost with a decision this significant.

Now, the fear is the only negative aspect of a tiny home that we won't be trying to fix. Rather, we'll simply focus on managing it. This is in part due to the fact that it's reasonable and healthy to have this kind of fear.

Getting into the world of tiny homes is a big leap of faith. It's important to understand exactly what you're getting into. Before you spend your first dime, you should have the whole operation planned out. Make sure every step is thoroughly planned, and your plans kept as safe as possible – that could be on paper or stored in a computer program, and so on.

Even then, dropping $30 000 in one shot is a stressful experience. No matter what you spend that kind of money on, you'll be feeling some doubts; it's simply inevitable. Even when doing more mundane things like buying a car, you'll feel stress before signing. Something that has helped many tiny home owners over the years knows that even if you only live in the home for four or five years, you'll be breaking even (or even coming out ahead) with paying rent.

Don't Get Too Fixated On Size

Now, something a lot of people do is fixate too much on the size of their tiny house. You don't need to adhere to some arbitrary number of square feet for your house to be considered "tiny."

Regardless of whether you go smaller or larger than the "common" definition of a tiny house, the project is still a great investment. The main reason to live in a tiny house is to form a connection with your place of living, as well as minimize spending.

This will result in a house that's quite a bit smaller than a regular one, but you don't need to be too extreme about it as long as you have space. Be realistic about your needs, and always keep children in mind.

Going a bit bigger to accommodate a larger family is perfectly fine. As is the inverse, making your tiny house even smaller than usual because you don't need the space.

Common Misconceptions

In this section, we'll be addressing some of the most common misconceptions and prejudices that tiny home owners will encounter. It's important not to approach these with a judgmental and superior outlook, but rather to discuss and argue against them reasonably.

Tiny Homes Are All Run-Down Cottages

This misconception is surprisingly common, especially given how few people have actually experienced a tiny home. While tiny homes can certainly be cottages, there's no reason for them to be any worse off than a regular home.

It's also worth noting that the time when most tiny homes were built from salvaged materials is far gone. Today, many tiny homes are made of the most modern and cutting-edge materials available.

Like with most things, tiny homes have the advantage of freedom here. We don't need to opt for cheap materials, nor do we need to shell out for the most expensive stuff out there. A tiny home is a means of expressing oneself. Using expensive materials is quite common.

Tiny Homes Are Messy

This is a myth; the likely cause lies in the misconception that we need to have a lot of things in our homes. When most people think about a tiny home, they're thinking about downsizing everything in their standard-sized home into a small space.

Naturally, if you put all that into a much smaller space in the same arrangement, it would look messy. Thankfully, this is not what tiny home owners do. The first thing to point out is that not every part of a standard-size house is actually necessary. For example, many homes have a few beds, couches, and sofas. A tiny house might instead only have one large bed and a couch. This is then applied to appliances, other furniture, and other objects.

The second thing is that tiny homes are very innovative when it comes to space management. In a standard-size house, you'll find that a lot of the space available is wasted.

Meanwhile, a tiny home will make the most of every inch of space available to it. Because of this, they tend to be more organized, not less. Disorganization is something that's extremely impractical for a tiny home, as you don't exactly have enough room to be disorganized.

Tiny Home Owners Are Snobby and Anti-Establishment

Some people develop feelings of animosity towards any group that even remotely looks like a subculture. This applies to most "niche" lifestyles. Some people feel like your every move is questioning their lifestyle, even if it might never occur to you.

Now, there's no denying that a lot of people living in tiny homes are rather passionate about the concept. For example, I'm literally writing a book about it. Naturally, people wouldn't have made a choice if they didn't feel like it was something they could feel proud of. With that being said, this doesn't make them arrogant.

This misconception is the reason why quite a few tiny home owners avoid talking about it. After all, if you don't want to be judged on your choices, you don't talk about them. Most of us are rather aware that the tiny home lifestyle won't mesh well with every individual, and that some people are better off with traditional housing.

With that being said, it's true that there's a community of people that own tiny houses. If you dislike that, nobody's putting pressure on you to join it; it's simply there if you want to.

The anti-establishment judgment comes from people who assume that the reason anyone would choose to live in a tiny house is to get away from Western society. While there are a thousand different words you could call someone that does this, "anti-establishment" seems to be a favorite. This descends from the fact that, well, quite a few that lived in tiny houses for a while were doing exactly that.

In this day and age, however, it's not possible to put that single label on all tiny house owners. This is because they've become widespread enough that they should no longer be associated with any kind of political ideology.

Now, while a lot of us do have the belief that the current prices of mortgages and similar "necessities" are way too large, that doesn't mean all of us to do. It should also be noted that this was a prevalent thought among many people way before this movement started.

Tiny Houses Lessen Property Values

This misconception is one that is, partially at least, due to the fact that most property owners and real estate brokers aren't very fond of the tiny house movement (it's rather bad for their profits.)

Now, one of the biggest selling points of living in a tiny home is usually how cheap it all is. A lot of our homes can be built for but a fraction of what a traditional house usually costs. This is usually considered to be a good thing; however, some in the zoning and building departments might see this as a very, very bad thing. They think that your tiny house will hurt the values of all of the properties around it. Otherwise, they might see it as only the first of many, each of which will eat into their profits more and more.

Now, if you keep your house orderly, and you act as a good neighbor to those around you, it's senseless to think that your very presence will drop the value of anything. Even if the presence of tiny houses did, in fact, bring down property values, it would take a whole lot more than one to do it.

Tiny Homes as Self-Expression

A tiny home is not only a place to live in, but it is also an almost art-like form. It can easily be a form of self-expression for you.

Most tiny home owners decide to make their own take on housing when they are making their home. Regardless of whether they're building it themselves, or having a company do it, they want to add their own spin to their home.

After all, why wouldn't they? Unlike a traditional home that has codes to abide by and fixed shapes that are almost certain, a tiny home can be whatever you want it to be! This freedom is what attracts many tiny home lovers to it.

After all, there are few other situations where you can affect your living environment on a reasonable budget. Due to the low area, you are also often able to choose materials that would be out of your budget if you were purchasing a home.

Now that we have that out of the way, let's look at the reasons why you should start living in a tiny home!

Chapter 2

Why Live In A Tiny Home?

One might think that we've listed out all of the pros and cons of living in a tiny home by now, but that's only partly true. While we've referenced most of the reasons one would migrate to a tiny home as opposed to a standard-sized one, we haven't delved very far into detail. We also haven't outlined many reasons why you wouldn't want to live in a tiny home.

The goal of this chapter is for you to consider all of the pros and cons of living in a tiny home. After all, owning a tiny home is a large commitment, and you'd do good to be as informed as possible when you make the call.

Pros of Living in a Tiny Home

It's Cheap

This is the most obvious benefit of living in a tiny home. It simply doesn't cost a lot. First of all, let's compare the prices of an average tiny home, and an average standard size home:

So, at an interest rate of 4.25%, a standard house in the US will set you back about $481 000, which is a lot of money. On the other hand, a tiny home will only cost you $23 000. This means that a tiny home costs only 5% of what a standard-sized one does.

Think about it this way, is the extra room you get really worth over $450 000? By purchasing a tiny home instead, you might be able to save up that amount, and who doesn't want an extra half-million in savings? Even if it's only in retirement money, it might mean retiring a few years earlier.

Looking past this, the price itself isn't the only way of living in a tiny home that is cheaper than a regular one.

The second most important element when it comes to price is furniture. Getting new furniture for a home can cost a small fortune. After all, there's so much space, what are you going to do, leave it empty? This kind of mindset often leads to people dropping thousands upon thousands of dollars on all kinds of furniture.

On the other hand, a tiny home doesn't need anywhere near that many pieces of furniture in it. Sure, you'll need a table (though usually a smaller one), a couch, a bed, and maybe a few chairs and drawers. But this is absolutely nothing compared to the amount of money that gets spent on furnishing a standard-sized apartment.

After coming to the bills, bills are something a few of us even though they were optional while living in standard-sized houses. For me personally, bills were an axiom of existence. Spending 20% of my monthly income on these additional expenses was perfectly normal.

22

Then came tiny homes. I no longer had to shell out that much of my income every month. Now, some tiny homes will be attached to the grid, and will, therefore, have some bills to pay. This is still nowhere near the amount a traditional home will.

This is mostly because of the small area. This, in turn, means there's less area that needs to be heated and cooled. Most small homes also filter their own water, leaving you with one less bill to pay. In case you're able to get a generator for electricity going, you'll be able to live completely free of bills!

Even if you give up on living in a tiny home after half a decade or so, you'll actually be gaining money, simply from not paying rent for that duration of time, as you'd have paid significantly more in rent than the cost of a small home.

You're Free to Move Where You Like

Freedom of movement is impossible to achieve with a traditional home (unless you're a millionaire.) Because of this, many people opt to take the tiny house approach. In fact, some tiny house owners also own a traditional home and use their tiny home for travel.

Being able to travel and bring your whole home with you is a great advantage. After all, it allows you to take a trip, and subtract all of the accommodation costs from it. Now, if you want to stay for a few days in a different city, this can easily knock a few hundred dollars off of your expenses.

On the other hand, if you're planning to stay for longer, then having a house you can move can be a lifesaver.

Another excellent option that living in a tiny home opens is the life of a digital nomad. So, while you can work online, being a digital nomad and travel around the world, it usually takes quite a bit of money. On the other hand, if you've got a tiny home, it takes basically none! Your only expense becomes the gas money necessary for you to take them home from point A to point B.

This means that the digital nomad lifestyle becomes available to a lot more people than it would otherwise be.

It's Easier to Maintain

Now, think about how much time it takes to do all the chores around a traditional home on an average day. Speaking optimistically, it takes at least an hour every day to finish cleaning, fixing broken appliances, etc. In a tiny home, this amount will be at most half.

Now, this might not seem like a lot at first. After all, what is half an hour more or less? To be fair, one day, it doesn't make much difference; however, the difference appears when you consider that this happens every day.

So, assuming you do chores for 30 minutes less for 40 years, you would have saved yourself 7300 hours! That is over 304 days; it's almost a year! So, if the prospect of saving almost a year's worth of time within your lifetime attracts you, a tiny home might be just the thing you need.

There are also fewer appliances and things that can get broken in a tiny home. This means you will spend less time and money on them. Thus leaving you with a lot more time to dedicate to hobbies and relationships.

It's Much Greener

In the 21st century, it's becoming more and more important to go green. In other words, one of the most important things we, as a people, can do is be as eco-friendly as possible. A tiny home is far superior to a traditional home when it comes to carbon footprint and general environmental friendliness.

A tiny home can also be moved to a less modernized area. By moving to a rural area, you make yourself feel closer to nature, which in turn helps us feel the responsibility for our planet and its future.

The first reason why tiny homes intrinsically do better for the environment is the size itself. Because tiny homes are smaller, that means they take a lot fewer materials to make than a traditional home would.

Furthermore, because they are smaller, that means they take up less space that could be filled with greenery. Then there's also energy consumption. A traditional home gets its power from the grid, which is usually at least in part based on using resources that are bad for the environment, such as coal or oil.

A lot of tiny homes are also made through the use of salvaged materials. This means that a tiny home most likely contains at least a few recycled materials. This is contrary to a traditional home that usually uses new materials for the whole construction.

Even if your tiny home isn't built by you, you'll still find that it's more eco-friendly when it comes to its construction. This is because most companies that build tiny homes are eco-conscious.

It Simplifies Things

This is possibly the most common reason why people opt to live in a tiny home. It is not the environmental consciousness; it is not the money; it's the desire to go back to a simpler time.

Today's world is complex. There is not one day that we do not encounter a variety of daily life's intricacies and problems. Most people simply get used to the chaos of everyday life.

With advertisers spamming us every few seconds, checking our phones every few minutes, and working for hours, it can be easy to lose oneself in the chaos. For many people, a tiny home is their anchor.

Having a simple, organized space helps people get into a simple, organized mindset. It is much like people with depression, cleaning their room to feel better. The simpler the area around you is, the more relaxed you'll feel. This is why tiny homes are great for people who lead chaotic lifestyles, such as CEO's or athletes.

A tiny home will also make you realize what is essential in your home and what is just...there. Many of us have shelves full of books that have been read or never will be. If you had a tiny home, you would have nowhere to put them, and would probably donate them to the city library.

Rather than keeping everything you don't need around "just in case" and cluttering your space, a tiny home makes you leave it behind and realize what really matters. A lot of people that live in tiny homes report feeling more confident and better about themselves.

Personalization

Another excellent benefit of a tiny home is the degree to which you get to personalize it. No two tiny homes are the same. If you're building it yourself, you get to personally design and build every aspect of the house.

This, in turn, means that you'll have a much more personal bond with space within. Because of this, whenever you enter, it'll feel much more "homey" than if it was just a house that you purchased as-is.

You can also add whatever additions you want, where ever you want. When you're buying a traditional house, the best you can do is settle for a house that most closely resembles what you want.

On the other hand, with a tiny house, you no longer need to settle for anything. You can make exactly what you want.

Easy Modifications and Appreciation of Space

Decorations and cosmetic modifications to a traditional house can last a whole week. Even just painting, it can be a full week's worth of chores. With a tiny house, you can easily paint it whole in a day.

Because there's less space in a tiny house, the few decorations you place during holidays pop out a lot more than they would on a larger house. Furthermore, you can make indoor modifications much easier, as every part of the house is easily accessible.

Furthermore, living in a tiny home really makes one appreciate space. It might sound a bit paradoxical, but living in a standard size house makes one more prone to wasting space. On the other hand, a tiny home makes sure that every inch is used to the best of its ability. Because of this, a tiny home can sometimes feel more spacious than a larger place (even though it's obviously not.)

Cons of Living in a Tiny Home

While the world of tiny homes has its obvious benefits, it's not without flaws. Now, this is not me saying that you shouldn't live in one, but rather that you should seriously consider whether or not you'll truly become happy by living in one.

This kind of lifestyle is not for everyone. Some people simply thrive best in a traditional environment. There is nothing wrong with that; however, it is better for you to find that out now than midway through building your tiny home.

So, without further ado, let's get into the bad sides of owning a tiny home:

You'll Have Less Space

Well, this one is pretty obvious. A tiny home, per definition, won't have the same amount of space that a larger one does. If you're someone that enjoys a large amount of space in your environment, then tiny homes definitely aren't for you.

But the issues don't only extend to empty space. Tiny homes make certain compromises, such as having smaller kitchen appliances than traditional houses. If you're someone that wants a luxury sized kitchen or bathroom, then a tiny home isn't for you.

Tiny home owners will often elect to ditch the bathtub, let alone having, say, a jacuzzi. Note that this also extends to storage space. If you like medium to large furniture or other items in your home, you'll have a hard time fitting them into the tiny house lifestyle.

This also applies in case your profession requires a lot of space. For example, a pianist who needs a full piano will have quite the issue fitting it into a tiny home. Before you get on with creating your tiny home, you need to ask yourself if you can really sacrifice the amount of space you'll need to.

It's Not Very Suitable for Families

While tiny houses on the larger side can sometimes be enough for a family of 3 or 4 people, most of them aren't. Tiny houses are ideal for one to two people. They even help foster the bond between them.

However, the moment you add more people into the equation, cracks start to show. At that point, the lack of space becomes an actual issue. Part of this is because you'll inevitably need to sacrifice a bit of kitchen/bathroom appliances. For example, a lot of tiny homes don't have washers and dryers, making them rely on laundromats to do their washing. For one or two people, this might be fine, but when it comes to a whole family, then it could cause a problem. For kitchen appliances, having only one or two stoves to cook on might not be enough.

Another issue is privacy. A tiny home simply doesn't give much room for privacy. While it may be a very comfortable home for one or two people, a family with children might find it hard to have their own space.

This is especially critical in the case of children, particularly teenagers. They need their privacy to do their homework and have fun with their friends. Unfortunately, this is a lot harder to do in a tiny home.

You Won't Be Hosting Any Large Parties

This is somewhat connected to the above point, but a tiny home simply doesn't have the capacity to hold that many people.

They promote a calm, almost solitary lifestyle. If you tried to bring two or three friends, you might be able to fit in. But a, say, ten people, Christmas dinner just isn't doable in the small space that a tiny home allows you.

Now, if your friends and family are alright with hanging out elsewhere, you can get around it. For example, having it at a relative's or even a restaurant. You'll find that in a way, living in a tiny home makes you more dependent on the outside world.

More Difficult Meal Prep

Preparing meals in advance is one of the big advantages of a traditional home. In a traditional home, you'll have a lot of space for a fridge, as well as for as many stoves as you need. This means that you'll have to cook for basically every meal.

Now, for some people who are used to cooking, this might not be a downside. On the other hand, if you aren't very fond of cooking, this will be a definite downside. You won't have much space to put your leftovers, so whatever you make, you'd better finish eating as well.

Heating and Cooling Can Be Harder

Now, this does depend on how your tiny home was built, but it can be quite difficult to heat up and cool off. This is mostly because most tiny homes won't have a very big AC unit. Because of this, if you live in an area with very warm summers (or very cold winters), you'll have issues with temperature management.

To remedy this, if you live in an environment with intense temperatures, you should ensure that the tiny home you're building has enough room on the upper walls for a big AC/heating unit. While it might use more energy, it'll be worth it.

Electricity and Plumbing Issues

In case you opt to generate your own electricity, usually using solar panels, you'll need to think about how you ration it. Things that use a lot of electricity, such as cooking or washing clothes will need to be timed for a while the sun is still out.

When it comes to plumbing, unless you opt for a fixed home, you'll have to use a composting toilet. This means that you'll have to empty your own waste every week or two. This can be rather troublesome for some people who would rather save themselves the smell.

In Recap

So, in essence, the biggest pro and con of a tiny home is one and the same- it is tiny. If you're someone that can't deal with small spaces, wants to host parties (or even children for that matter,) then a tiny home probably isn't the thing for you.

On the other hand, if what you want is a place that's easy to maintain, eco-friendly, and simple, then a tiny home is your friend. Personalization is, once again, king, so there's a chance that you could get around most of the cons if you built your house a specific way. With that being said, cons that are derived from the lack of space will never go away.

Chapter 3

Design - What You Need to Know?

Designing a tiny home can seem like a rather daunting task at first. Though these homes come at a much lower price, they are just as good as a regular house, just more eco-friendly. If you are looking for something to make truly your own, I've got some good news for you. Despite the limitations of a tiny home, they are extremely customizable. Or, rather, they encourage you to make something unique to you, due to the aforementioned limitations. Working with a limited amount of space means that you will have to really think about how you are going to use every millimeter. Now, while this prospect might seem intimidating, you should not be afraid. It is all a part of your own unique journey. By carefully thinking about using your own space, you will feel as if your tiny home is a part of yourself and something that you can really love and care for.

So, What Are My Options?

Of course, when you are building your own house, the sky's the limit. You can design it how you want it, and find the most efficient solutions for you. However, this is a fickle prospect. While it is true that this method of obtaining a new home will help you grow closer to it and make it mean more to you, it comes with all sorts of risks and responsibilities. Even the finest of craftsmen have trouble building a house that takes up minimal space, yet provides you with everything you need. You really need to know what you are doing; otherwise, you might be endangering yourself. Building a tiny home is not as easy as it sounds, but that's why there are companies that can do that for you.

Selecting a Company

While you might think that getting your tiny home from a company will take away from its value, I assure you that it will not. Recently, there have been more and more providers of this service.

For example, Tumbleweed provides such services. If you have never heard of them, you surely have heard of their mantra: "Dream Big, Go Tiny," and they make good on it. Tumbleweed has been a leader in the field since 1999. They have been building residential RVs for a very long time and are professionals. Their name is stamped with many certificates and will hold up no matter what.

They are also very easy to work with. You will get many feedback sessions, and they will always try to implement your every want and need as efficiently as possible. They specialize in rustic interior design. They use wood for most of their construction, and they make it incredibly presentable. The houses are also extremely spacious, often including a smaller upper floor that is used as a bedroom. The designs this company provides will not let you down. If all of the wood chopping worries you, fret not. The company provides a very eco-friendly solution in the form of Green Recreational Vehicles. The prices for constructing this kind of house range from 69,000-92,000 USD. While this might seem a bit much, remember that it includes the costs of planning, materials, as well as construction. Of course, if this might look like too much of an investment, the company offers plenty of insurance policies, as well as a 23-year payment plan. Deals as good as this rarely come this cheap.

If you are looking for something more modern, as well as more customizable, you should look no further than New Frontier. New Frontier works under a very simple set of rules. They aim to make proper housing as affordable as possible. The company has 40 years of experience. For these 40 years, they aimed to improve many lives by bringing affordable design and economic freedom to their buyers. This company is very old in the field, and its longevity only speaks for its success. If you are looking for luxury and sustainability, this should be your go-to. The downside is that this deal comes at a price that's a bit steeper than most others. Their projects start off at 95,000 USD. On the other hand, this is a relatively low price when it comes to luxurious housing. These houses are extremely customizable, and you will rarely find a company with more options than this one.

If you are looking for options while making your home, look no further than 84 Lumber's Tiny Living. What's so special about 84 Lumber it that they are fast and efficient. They are also extremely cheap. When working with the company, you will be offered three options. The three options differ from one another based on the price. If you are looking to build your home on your own, their DIY option starts at 7,000 USD. A semi-DIY option starts at 20,000 USD, while their move-in ready option starts at 50,000 USD. They offer four different house models. All of them are under 210 square feet. This helps you minimize your environmental footprint, as well as inspire a sense of wanderlust. All of the four models are equipped with their own unique features. All of them include move-in ready amenities. If you are looking for fast and efficient, this is the choice for you as they guarantee that the house will be built within ten weeks.

Escape Traveler is another great choice. It is ideal for locations in extreme climates. Most of their design always focuses on letting sunlight in, giving a feeling of openness and connection to your surroundings. These tiny homes boast an incredibly beautiful kind of architecture. They will have a lot of windows on the doors, walls, and even the roof to give you more light. It is just so hard not to fall in love with this kind of house. It is just charming in all kinds of ways. What nobody can deny is how meticulous Escape Traveler is when making tiny homes. Every single house they have built simply exudes love for good craftsmanship and aesthetics. Their houses are not too expensive, either. Their prices range from 39,000 USD to 79,000 USD. A variety of choices are available to you when it comes to customization; however, they are limited by your location.

One of the lesser-known, but loved companies that deal in tiny homes is Pin-Up Houses. They are extremely stylish, having a very modern look to them despite how simple their designs are. While Pin-up Houses does not work with assembly and delivery, they sell incredibly slick construction plans. The plans cost 29 US dollars, and if that does not seem safe enough to you, they come with a money-back guarantee. Their most popular model is the Cheryl Cabin. This little abode can be constructed for around 3,000 US dollars. It spreads over 107-square feet with a porch that gives you another 47 square feet. The house is designed to be a vacation retreat, and for that cost, you will find very few tiny houses that will be better than this one.

One of the many good sides of owning a tiny home is how eco-friendly they are. If this is your priority, you will find a friend in Wheelhaus. Wheelhaus has one simple motto: "Less is more." This includes all of the aspects of your new home: fewer materials, less time, less waste. The houses produced by Wheelhaus do something amazing. They fuse the modern and the rustic extremely well. While looking at the architecture of these houses, you will notice how incredibly the two elements mold. The usage of space in relation to humble wooden ornaments will always be a joy to look at.

While it might seem as if they are fragile due to their surface construction, I assure you they are not. They are as durable as any log cabin, just without the burliness. How durable are they? Well, notably, they can withstand incredibly strong winds, as well as powerful snowfall. They come equipped with numerous additions that will make your life much better. The insulation of these tiny homes is incredible, to say the least. The "less is more" motto, however, does not apply to their windows, doors, and ceilings. These houses are notably spacious despite the relatively small surface they take up. They also make relatively good use of natural lighting to bring out the beauty of the interior design. While you are in one of them, you will rarely feel like you are in a small house. Rather, they almost feel like mansions. "Then the delivery must be slow and hard to execute." you might say. That, however, is not true. Wheelhaus prides itself on the efficiency of their deliveries. The houses are, however, a tad bit pricy.

These homes most often cost somewhere between 80,000 and 125,000 USD. On the other hand, they are more than well worth it. Wheelhaus's tiny homes will definitely feel like homes, not just small houses.

Whichever tiny home kit you opt for, there are several things that you should remember at all times. The common denominator for all of these houses is the fact that they are always somewhere between 100 and 400 square feet. This might seem like a huge surface, but you will see that it is not. You can get the maximum out of little floor space by going for height, but the space for appliances will not be superfluous. This is why many tiny houses go for a layered design, having "pseudo floors." Often, your rooms will often be one single space. Your bathroom will often be not far away from the place where you make your food. If you require spacing out for personal reasons, this might not be for you. On the other hand, multitasking will be much easier than in other houses.

A lot of tiny homes are designed to be portable. This is a big part of the charm of tiny homes. You have heard the old proverb: "Home is where the heart is," and now, home is wherever you go. Isn't it great? When going on a trip, or even moving to a different town, often people get homesick. They start missing their bread, their favorite lamp, the wall they used to stick notes to. Well, now, that is not a problem. Your house goes with you wherever you go. You will never again have to sleep without a favorite pillow. It almost seems like a dream, doesn't it?

Most of the newer tiny homes can be moved with a pickup truck or even a car. The only thing you need to consider in your new location is finding a place to land your home. However, not every tiny home is like this. Some of them are heavy enough that they require a crane to be placed on a platform. Others cannot even be moved, requiring a foundation to be built. It is often hard to decide what kind of tiny home you want. You should always first consider what kind of mobility you are looking for. This will help you narrow down your options quickly.

What people often forget is that tiny home, like most buildings, needs land. Even while they aren't tied down to foundations, there is still the issue of placing it somewhere. While it might be idyllic just to place it wherever you find some free space, this is not how it works. However, there are several solutions if you need them.

The first option is to find someone renting their backyard. Portable tiny houses do not count as buildings, rather "accessory dwelling units." This means that you can place your home in the backyard of anyone looking to get some rent money.

Renting land is also an option. When you are not looking towards permanence in a location, this is a great choice as you can go away whenever you feel like it.

When we are talking about houses with a foundation, buying your own piece of land is, of course, an option. However, this can be extremely expensive, often breaking your bank and putting you in debt. Similarly to renting land, this will, however, give you an incredibly large backyard as these kinds of parcels are made for bigger houses.

There are some communities dedicated to finding more people like you. You can find them on the web whenever you need them. However, remember that they will often have different rules when it comes to renting and living, as well as living within the community. Again, this, too, is mostly a thing of your preferred mobility.

Building a Tiny Home

Building a tiny home is a whole other game, however. Professionals often have years of experience behind them, and your new home will look like another Thursday evening to them. You are not a pro, however, and designing your paradise can be quite intimidating. To be certain, it is a job for those with the toughest of nerves. It is a stressful thing to do. There are so many things to consider, so many little moving pieces that need to work in perfect unison. And, just to make it even more stressful, one slight mistake can ruin everything. You can, of course, always hire a professional to design your new home, but this costs money,+ and you don't get the experience. You want your house to be yours. Something you made from scratch and professional help just will not do. That being said, here are a few things to consider, as well as a few techniques that will make this endeavor more manageable.

Of course, the first thing that you should do is make sure that you got to know the surface you are working with. This is extremely important when you are building a static house. Building foundations is never an easy task. This is because so many things can go wrong. The land can be very uneven, and the ground can be shallow under the surface. This can be catastrophic for your project. Wetlands can always be a problem. It can also be problematic to avoid them. Besides that, there are other things that you should consider, like flooding. If the area you are planning to build on is known for floods, you are going to have to make a lot of adjustments to your plans.

The best thing you can do before starting to build your dream home is to find out what other people did while doing the same thing as you. This is also the best way to find a starting point. Learning from other people's successes and failures will help you immensely. This will speed up the time you need to finish your project, and it will give you more confidence as your actions have worked for people before you.

Another thing that you should do as soon as possible is to find help. Professionals are always an option, but it is easy to assume that this does not interest you. If you have some friends and family that are willing to help you, the job will be much faster and much easier. While it is much harder to organize more people than just yourself, the job is best done while you aren't alone. This will make the experience more fun too. Sharing the joy of making your home with people that you consider closer to you will make it even more special.

It is important to remember that this is not something that can be done quickly. While it might be tempting to try to fool yourself by thinking that everything will go according to plan, things are bound to pop up from time to time. The time needed to finish up will also be extremely unpredictable. Do not let yourself be discouraged by this. That is, by far, the most important advice you can get. Do not get discouraged. A lot of things can go wrong, and it is easy to give up with even the slightest of missteps, you should never give up. This whole ordeal can be seen as a test of character.

The first thing you should do is get a feel of the space. This can be done with a lot of duct tape or anything else that you can suspend from one point to another. How does this work? It's simple. Stand in the space that you are going to use, take your tape or string or whatever you are using to do this and mark every bit of space that is going to be used in your design. What this does is give you a feel for space. It gives you a general idea of how you will have to move to your new home and how much space you wasted/have left. It is a great method of getting closer to your design without committing to anything. If you just toss up a plan and follow it through, it will soon be too late to realize that you made a mistake. From that point on, going back will be very costly and stressful. And what you really don't want is your dream house turning into a nightmare.

Another thing that you will need to always think about is how to use your furniture efficiently. While yes, a lot of furniture can be used for multiple things that are not exactly what I am aiming for. Fold-down furniture is a great thing for tiny home enthusiasts. While you might not be able to do this with most furniture, do it with what you can. For example, tables and desks are a great way to save space. A dining table will take up a lot, and this can be quite a problem. Now imagine being able to fold that table into the floor or a wall while you are not using it. Can you imagine how much space it will open up? Suddenly, one of the biggest downsides of owning a tiny home becomes much less of a problem. The best thing about this is that it is easy to do on your own. You just need a few hinges and some mechanical knowledge to make something like this.

Similarly to that, walls can be used for multiple purposes as well. If you are going to have a lot of things going on inside your house, you have to make proper use of your walls and floor. The first example you might think of is the kitchen. Even in regular houses, you will try to find ways to hang items on the walls to save space and make them more approachable. This makes the mess you might make more manageable and gives you more drawer space for things that you cannot place on your wall. Alternatively, if you can, repurpose as many walls as possible into shelving. While this might seem like a small thing, think of it as another book or decoration that you get to keep. Another thing to keep in mind when it comes to storage is that it is a good idea to keep as much of it as possible below your waist. This will give you a sense of openness to your home and will give you more room to move your arms without getting hurt.

When making plans for your new home, it is smart to make your ceilings as high as possible. This not only gives you more space to move around, but it also helps space feel larger and more comfortable. It also allows for more windows to be built in. This will let in more natural light, making your house look even prettier. On top of this, low-sitting furniture is something you should also consider. Again, it gives a sense of openness to your home and makes it lighter on the eyes.

There are several more ways to give your home a roomier feel. Other than installing a lot of windows, you should use lighter colors for the interior. Another way to do this is by using mirrors. By doing this, you give the illusion of making the room look bigger. It is also very useful. You will always want a mirror that you can use to look at yourself while getting ready.

If you are looking to expand what your home can do, it is smart to make any space that has several different functions. This is important due to the limitations you work under. People often think that adding things like a guest room is impossible; however, having some chairs in your dining room that can be flipped over to be used as a bed. Alternatively, you can use your couch as a bed, as well as a place where you can work on your computer whenever you might need it.

Using your couches as an additional storage area is also an option. You can always put some clothes under the cushions. You do this to be able to keep as many things as possible that are not necessary. A pair of clothes or a book you like will always bring a smile to your face. However, you should keep in mind the fact that there is a limit to how far you can take this. If you take it too far, doing a lot of your day-to-day activities can become an unnecessary challenge.

If you are looking for more space, you can also build a home with a basement. This is impossible with portable tiny homes, however. Luckily, there is a way to store your things under the floor. Double floors are pretty rare, but they aren't the strangest thing ever and involve building the floor in such a way that it has two layers. The lower layer is the one that divides your home from the ground. The upper one is several inches above the first one, suspended by grids that are connected to the walls. If you want to go for something like this, a wooden floor is a must. You won't be able to do it with any other material. This will be quite difficult to build into your home, but if you manage to do it, it opens a completely new dimension to your home. It will help you have a lot of space when space is needed and gives you space for things you won't need soon. The limitation is that you will not be able to store large things, but hey, the alternative is not being able to store anything under the floorboards.

When you design your home, you should avoid partitioning as much as possible. You do not have the luxury to have more walls than necessary. The only walls that are acceptable are those that are separating the interior of your home from the exterior. This is the only way that you can make your room, office, and living room into one single space. However, if you feel as if partitioning is necessary and you need more than one room, you should use sliding walls as much as possible. This helps you deal with the problem of privacy. Even when you do not need privacy, the sliding walls will make your home feel much bigger than it actually is.

There is another layer of things to consider when making a mobile home. While you will mostly make a house that can be moved, a lot of people will opt for making a house that moves. The difference is small but not ignorable. There are houses that are foundationless houses that sit at the top of a grassy hill. When you want to move this house somewhere, you will need a crane to place it on top of a moving platform, and then you carefully move it from location A to location B. Houses that move are houses that are built on wheels. These are usually built around RVs or Caravans.

While caravans and RVs have always been a sort of an image for houses on wheels, this time, I mean it literally. People often tear down the construction of a caravan, only keeping the basic elements. After this, you base your plans on what remains of the caravan and then build around it. This limits your creative capabilities but cuts down a part of your work.

If you enjoy this idea, there are several more things that you have to keep in mind. The first is that you should never start moving to a new house before you are one hundred percent sure of what you have built. Your house collapsing or getting a chunk to fall off is bad while it is placed on the land. These events are much worse while you are moving at high speeds on a highway. Safety should always come first. Once you make your house, get a professional to check it out. If you get a green light, the world is your oyster.

Building on the foundations of a vehicle can be limiting in many ways. The surface area you are working with is extremely limited. While it CAN be expanded, there are limits to how much you can do so safely.

On top of this, you are going to have to build a system that is self-reliable. A generator will be necessary if you are going to use a lot of electronics inside your home. If you do not want to go to the nearby gas station every time you need to use the bathroom, you are going to have to go for a plumbing system that anchors itself on a pair of reservoirs that you need to fill up and empty out regularly. The weight of the materials is another limitation. The base of your RV or caravan can hold out only so much. The same can be said for the vehicle that is pulling your home. This also excludes several material options when it comes to the interior. Any bit of furniture that is tied down is just another problem that you will eventually have to deal with. Heavy ceramic tiles will also be problematic as they break relatively easy, on top of giving you a lot of weight.

Decorations are something that you are going to be humble with. They take up a lot of space and provide no specific use. While decorating is the main way you can customize your home and put some "you" into it. However, your options when it comes to this are limited. Keep that in mind, while planning out your project.

Yet another issue may arise in places where you need a special permit for your mobile home. The law, when it comes to this subject, is not the same wherever you may go. Make sure to see if a permit is necessary and if so, get the permit. While it is an additional cost, it will keep you out of unnecessary trouble in the future.

Do not go too crazy with your design. Having smaller foundations in the ground or on top of a vehicle not only gives you less space, but it also gives you fewer spots where you can place core elements of your construction. This means that you are going to have to hold back when it comes to shaping your home. While it might be tempting to have your home look more modern by adding a few spaces that go over the square that you were originally built on, try not to. The thing is that most of your core elements will be much weaker (due to their size) and that they will be problematic to place just anywhere you want. If you want to modify the exterior shape of your home, you should always talk to a professional before doing so. There are just too many things that can go wrong, and if they do, they will cause a domino effect across your home. Make sure that your home can handle your additions before doing them. Build smart and not pretty.

If you are looking to build your tiny home out of a shipping container, there are a few more things to think about. Like every other tiny home solution, it comes with both ups and downs. You will be able to find a container for as low as a few thousand dollars. This is great due to the fact that on its own, it makes up the entirety of your main construction. Containers are usually very durable and waterproof, eliminating some potential problems. You will also be doing nature a favor. Containers are usually very difficult to recycle, so they are just piled onto a junkyard. By making this conscious decision, you are both using a good resource for a good purpose and are keeping garbage away from the outside world. Containers also come with the amazing benefit of being stackable. This means that if you ever want to expand or elevate your home in the future to make it more comfortable for your family, you can do so relatively easily. Something that can be said for all of the tiny homes made from containers is that they look pretty modern. The shape and material of your home will give it an incredibly moldable aesthetic and, with a bit of paint and some additional decor, you will easily turn it into something unique. The issue of the security of your house is covered by the robust nature of containers themselves. Due to the material, your house will be very difficult to damage and even more difficult to break into. Containers do not come with built-in windows, so you can use this to your advantage.

However, a home does need windows. You need natural lighting as much as your home does. It is no secret that lighting makes all the difference when it comes to the aesthetics of the interior, and just by using it, you can give a completely new look to your home. Having a lot of natural sunlight will benefit you, as well. However, building windows on the sides of containers is not the easiest task ever. Actually, changing the structure of a container in any way, shape, or form, such as adding partitions, requires a professional to get involved. This is because it is easy to jeopardize the structure of the container, potentially turning it into a hazardous environment. They will also give you less space by proxy. I mean, if you compare a container to an RV, the difference will usually not be that big, but when you are already working with limited space, the issue of the several inches that you would get from an RV might be extremely important. Another problem arises with heating control. As you might know, the relatively thin sheets of metal that make up a container make it so that winters will be extra cold and that summers will be extra hot. This does not go to the extent of it being uncomfortable to be inside of your home; rather, it can be very dangerous and potentially life-threatening to fall asleep inside of a container that is poorly insulated during summer. You are going to have to be very careful and meticulous with insulation, as it can make or break your project.

If you opt to go for a container tiny home, you follow most of the steps as you usually would. You carefully design your home, keeping everything that might be important in mind. It is as important as ever, if not more, to have an engineer look at your plan. This is because containers are very tricky to deal with from an architectural standpoint, and you really do not want to mess it up. After that, you select your container or containers. The beauty of containers is how easily you can combine them. You can place them atop one another to save some surface area of your land. You just cut an opening that connects them, and there you go. There is one additional step when talking about this type of tiny home. The floors of shipping containers are often treated with strong chemicals. They can be potentially harmful, so it is a good idea to remove the floor or add a sub-floor to keep yourself away from said chemicals. The rest of the steps are the same as with any other home. Gather materials, hire or call for help, build it, decorate it, and move in.

Make sure that you decide which materials you will use up-front. This will help you gather them more efficiently and will save you a few unnecessary trips. It will also let you have a piece of your future project which you can go off from. When you decide what kind of roof you want, it helps you know what kind of wall you are going to want and what additional hardware you are going to need. Knowing what kind of flooring you are going for will help you get the wood that goes the best with it and will let you know what kind of binding you will need.

Chapter 4

Building-What Materials Will I Need?

Again, it is important to mention that, if you are not a good craftsperson, this endeavor will be a very difficult one. While the architecture is far simpler than in a larger home, a tiny home has a relatively fragile construction. A lot can go wrong and, if you are not ready for it, it can be quite a catastrophe. That being said, hiring a professional company, as mentioned before, is always an option. However, there will always be the question of providing materials for the building of your home. As you might imagine, it isn't all about bricks and cement. While it can be, this would go against the eco-friendliness of your project. You will see many similarities with building a regular house, but with some additions and exclusions that go toward practicality.

Wood and Portability

The first thing that you should think about is if you want your tiny home to be portable. If the answer is "no," you just follow the procedure that you would follow with regular houses. You build a foundation (though it is not necessary), and you go from there. If you want your home to be portable, though, there is something that you need to consider at great length. You will probably be using wood for most of your construction. However, you can't just use any piece of wood. There is a matter of weight that you need to take into consideration. Usually, it is smart to use as light of wood as you can to avoid difficulties with transportation. While drywall might seem like a good idea, trust me, it isn't. It is far too heavy and not durable enough. Even strong winds might be enough to damage it.

While we are on the subject of durability, make sure that you choose the wood that fits your surroundings. For example, if you live in an area where rain falls often, you want wood that is very water-resistant. On top of that, you want wood that keeps in heat as much as possible and rots as slowly as possible. However, with proper maintenance and additional insulation, neither of these two will be a problem. Of course, there is never any guarantee, so I suggest that you have a chat with a professional in the field.

Like with any construction project, you are going to need a basis to build on. The first few things you should get are the basic elements of your construction. Dimensional lumber is the first element. This is already prepped for construction and is a good start. Be careful, though, as the dimensions are often misleading. For example, a 4x5 will be 3.5 inches by 4.5 inches.

Plywood is another important element. This wood is very durable and is a key part of your construction as it can and will hold most of the weight of your house. However, it can be a bit pricey, so you have some cheaper alternatives. For example, OSB (oriented strand board). The downside of OSB is that it is heavier and much less durable than plywood.

Your walls will be built out of two layers most of the time. The inside layer should be built from light and durable materials. Most of the time, you will use sheet paneling. The outside layer, as mentioned before, needs to be resistant to the elements, while still not being too heavy. The kind of wood most often used for this is cypress and cedar.

Insulation

While at the subject of protection from the elements, insulation is an important part of any construction project. There is no debate about that. What good is a house that cannot be lived in during the entire winter? Styrofoam is an incredible thing, you see. You will mostly use it to insulate your subfloors. While this is the main use, it is not uncommon for it to be used to insulate the roof and walls as well.

A few cans of spray foam will be necessary as well. You will use it to fill in the tiny spaces between the smaller elements of your building, namely windows and doors. You need to know your foams to use it efficiently. There are slight differences that can be very important. If you use foam that expands too much, you risk your windows and doors not working properly. This is because the jambs can bend too much and stop functioning as they should. You will need a huge amount of foam if you are going to use Styrofoam as part of your insulation. Moisture can often be a problem with mainly wooden constructions. However, by using Housewrap, you create a sort of barrier that helps you maintain the strength of your wood, as well as add a little bit more insulation to your house. There are a lot of different companies that produce house wrap, so I recommend looking into the brands before purchasing. While this might not seem like a big deal, it is. You will need a special kind of tape to seal the spaces between your layers of house wrap. You can find this tape in most hardware stores.

Roofing

Roofs are the symbols of home when you think about it. How often do you hear the phrase: "Under my roof..."? Well, as you may imagine, roofing is extremely important. It keeps you secluded from the natural elements and literally puts a roof over your head. While tiles are something we take for granted in roofing, with tiny homes, it is not as easy. While yes, the gorgeous scale-like red rooftops are something that we are all very used to, they just do not work on a tiny home, especially one that is built for moving. They are both very heavy and are a potential additional cost as they might need replacement down the line. Fortunately, there is a cheap and relatively easy solution.

When building a roof for your tiny home, you are looking for simple and reliable. That is why you always go for metal roofing. Why? The answer to that is very simple. You see, metal will give you the most durable roofing in relation to weight. This is very important when you are looking to transport your home. Due to the harsh conditions, your home will be placed under during transportation, being able to sustain as little damage is very important. Metal is, as we all know, extremely durable. However, it comes with one more upside. In the case of damage, it is the easiest to replace. While it is true that you might need to replace a huge portion of your roof due to just a little bit of damage, this will be very easy to do, as well as relatively cheap. While you might think that metal roofing is unattractive, I assure you it can be made into something pleasant for the senses.

There isn't a huge variety of colors that you can choose from, but the gray can be very appealing on its own. Metal also gives you incredibly diverse options for the shape of your roof and decorations. Unfortunately, you will rarely find metal roofing being sold as it is. This is because it is not something commonly used, so you will have to purchase the individual elements and assemble them as you go. However, even without a professional craftsperson, this will not be too hard to do. However, it is best that you find a local manufacturer that can tailor it to your needs. All roofing needs underlayment, and that's where tar paper comes into play. There is not much that you can say about it, as different brands of tar paper provide very little difference. However, if you are not afraid of dishing out a bit more money, Ice and Rain shields do the same job. The main difference is that Ice and Rain shields are way more durable and have a longer lifetime. It is also backed by adhesive, making it much easier to install. Again, the material your roof is made of comes into play here. If your roof is metal, you should buy shields that are adjusted for high temperatures. We all know how hot metal construction elements get during summer.

Make Sure You're Using the Right Hardware

It would be redundant to stress the importance of hardware, so a short run-down should be enough. People often forget the importance of using proper hardware. It is easy to forgo small parts and just use regular nails and screws for everything, but I assure you, doing things by the book, though more expensive, is going to do you a favor in the long run. Regular screws will do just fine for the exterior elements. Assuming you are using wood, they will keep your house in one piece without much effort. The little twist comes with the roof. Again assuming that you use metal roofing, you should get metal nails that come with a butyl backed washer. These nails can easily pierce through the roofing, meaning that no drilling will be required beforehand and that the hole will be sealed tightly enough that no water can get through. Heavy-duty nails will also be required to secure the snapping. You will, of course, need some backers, nuts, and bolts for your subfloor. As you may imagine, the more fragile and thinner parts of your construction like tar paper are not something that can just be hammered down with any nails. Plasticap nails come with a large plastic head that can secure elements like that more tightly while risking less damage. Brads and finishing nails are necessary to put in the finishing pieces that you might not with regular nails. They are much longer and are used to secure things like casing. Do not forget to get some nail plates as well. These metal plates are placed along with your piping or other fragile elements of your house to avoid damage while using brads or nails.

While building in areas that are known for strong winds, you are going to need some hurricane straps. The reason you see roofs getting torn off houses during strong winds is due to the angle between the walls and the roof. This is where these straps come into play. They reinforce the linkage between the wall and rafter, giving your construction that additional resilience that you might want or need. H clips are something you will want in every metal construction. Your roof will often be a product of several layers of metal. These layers cannot be hugging each other too tightly as, while metal expands and contracts due to the natural elements. If there is not enough space between the layers of metal, you risk serious damage. We're talking potentially life-threatening damage. The first function of H clips is to give the metal the space it needs to breathe. The second function is letting the sheets of metal reinforce one another better. You will need different kinds of flashing as well. Flashing is a material that is used to keep water away from your wood. We all know what kind of effect water has on wood, and we always want to prevent it. Not all flashing is the same, and you should ask around your hardware store before making a purchase.

Electricity

Providing electricity to your home is a bit trickier. I recommend hiring a professional to do this, but if you are steadfast in doing it yourself all the way, here are a few things you should know. Of course, you know the basic elements of electric wiring. All wires are the same when it comes to function, but always aim for endurance, no matter the cost. A home needs to be not only comfortable but also safe. We do not want to put our loved ones or ourselves into danger. Something that you should never forget about is wire staples. I know that it seems basic enough, but keeping them in mind will save you one or more trips to the hardware store. They are hammered in and serve the purpose of keeping your wires where they are supposed to be. Wiring can be an extreme hazard, so you best be wary of how you approach it.

Plumbing

Plumbing, of course, is just as important. Having a proper place to wash will always be one of your priorities. While it is a commodity of a sort, water inside of our homes has become such an underappreciated part of our lives. You will need different kinds of pipes for water supply and drainage. It is best to ask around a hardware store as different kinds of pipes are available in different places. If you are looking for a quick-to-build shower, it is best to go for a one-piece fiberglass one. It is light and relatively easy to maintain and does not take up a lot of space. These are all of the things you want from all of your commodities. The quality of the water heater is something that people often overlook as well. It is just as important of an element as anything else inside of your house. That being said, getting a small heater is a must. You just cannot afford the space required for a regular-sized one. On top of that, you should always make sure that it has internal heating, as it prevents it from freezing when it gets really cold.

Tiling

Tilling, while being the last thing to install, is extremely important for the general aesthetic of your home. Hardwood flooring is always a great option. It is very pretty to look at and comes in so many different colors and patterns. Of course, you should never place hardwood in areas like your bathroom, as water can ruin them extremely quickly. Tile is a very popular flooring for bathrooms and kitchens. Water does little to nothing to it, and, again, it is very easy on the eyes. One thing you should take into consideration, however, is how heavy tiles are. This can cause you a lot of trouble when transporting your home. Something that can also happen during transport is for your tiles to crack. There are several different materials that tiling can be made from porcelain and vinyl. Vinyl does have way fewer options when it comes to design, but more than makes up for it with its durability and how easy it is to install. Of course, you will also need adhesive. The kind of adhesive you are going to have to use will depend on what flooring you are going for. When making a purchase, ask the people working in the hardware shop; they will give you a general idea of what your options are.

Additional Options

If you are going for a portable house, some of your needs will change. First of all, your wiring will have to be connected to a generator that is installed in your house. If you are going for greenness and cost efficiency in the long run, solar panels are always an option. Your plumbing will also drastically change. You are going to need a freshwater tank, a water pump, and a grey tank (for waste disposal).

When it comes to heating and conditioning, you are free to go for whatever option you might like. Just make sure that you are using as little space as possible.

Of course, there are ways to cut down your costs. If you are going for an extremely budget DIY solution, there are ways you can do this. There have been records of people building their tiny homes for incredibly low prices by using discarded materials. This is the pinnacle of eco-friendly construction. You can repurpose many things as parts of your home. Visiting the local junkyard can help you keep your budget up, and it helps your community, not by much, but it helps. You can get metal panels that you can use for your roofs. Old wooden pallets can be used as parts of your walls, as well as bits of your floor. You can go as far as making your own furniture from such materials. For example, you can make a comfy bed by using a palette and placing a few pillows and a mattress over it. While not the most comfortable thing in the world, it is extremely cost-efficient. You can use the frames of old paintings as window frames. This, while not the most efficient thing ever, will do the job as well as you need it to be done. This might be the best and the worst option for you, depending on how handy you are and what your budget is.

Have you ever heard of Binishells? They can be used as an argument for the fact that tiny homes have been around for much longer than you think. Dante Bini invented them during the 60s. While he was alive, he built 1,600 of them. To be fair, they were not originally made to serve a residential purpose. Rather, they were imagined to be shelters in case of emergency or classrooms. Be it as it may, as of recent, they have been a growing trend in the community of tiny home enthusiasts. Why? Because they are extremely easy and fast to build. The method requires some pretty advanced and expensive equipment, which makes sense as they were originally planned to be mass-produced. However, this way of building a house is extremely cost-effective, which is one of the main reasons it is so popular. How does the method work? It is quite simple actually, believe it or not. Have you ever covered a balloon with papier-mache?

If you have, then you have a general grasp of how this works. Just replace the balloon with a heavy-duty bladder that is tied to an air pump. After that, the bladder, now surrounded by steel rebar, is covered by concrete. After this, the bladder is deflated. Once this is done, you have your home ready to be moved into. Yes, it is that simple. The process is unbelievably fast, and the house is incredibly resilient. It has been reported to be immune to strong winds, earthquakes, or things as crazy as lava flows. With all of this, it is easy why binishells started becoming so popular. Fast, safe, and effective, building one can cost as little as 4,500 US dollars. The architecture, though simple, can make for a pretty sight as well.

A lot of people have done this. You can find articles that detail their journeys on the internet. For example, a woman named Macy Miller underwent such a task. She bought an old RV for 500 US dollars and started building from there. She turned this RV into a beautiful home for just 12,000 dollars. Impressed? Wait till you hear the rest of it. Over the course of two years, she turned it into a comfortable 196-square-foot family house. You might be thinking that there is no way that a family could live in 196 square feet, but you could not be more wrong. Through careful planning, Macy Miller made a home that now hosts her husband, her, their child, and a huge Great Dane. Other than being a family home, it is also a great place to live in. It has radiant floor heating, meaning that winters and autumns are not a problem. The house also comes equipped with a few eco-friendly additions like a composting bathroom. Macy Miller is one of the many people who proved that you could make a comfortable tiny home for a small amount of money.

Another incredible solution came from Dave Herrle. He built a treehouse as part of a promise he made to his wife on New Year's Eve. To show just how much of an incredible craftsman Herrle is, he built the house in a matter of six weeks. If that is not impressive enough, he did so for an incredibly low 4,000 US dollars. While this might seem crazy and farfetched, I assume that it is not. The crazier part is that he did so on a hillside by using two trees. This is an incredible project, as it takes the most creative of us to think of something like this. A tiny treehouse that you can live in just fills you with childish wonder. This might seem like something weird, but as of late, this has started getting more and more common. Treehouses have started growing in popularity among tiny home enthusiasts, and it is easy to see why. They are both stylish and comfortable. On top of that, they are extremely low-maintenance, especially if you use natural wood. Dave's home looks over the woods from a hillside. It has aluminum roofing that will last him a long time as well.

When it comes to budget tiny home construction, I think that we have a definitive winner in Scott Brooks. Scott set out to make a home for just himself and nobody else. He built a tiny home that covers 83 square feet. He did it all on his own. However, this is not the impressive part. He did this for only 500 dollars. You might think that this is impossible or, if possible, you will probably assume that the house is not as good as you might want it to be. However, Scott did an amazing job. He did an incredible thing when it comes to cutting down the costs of building his home. He used salvaged materials to make everything in his home. And I mean everything. The front side of his home hosts a door and a large window. The large window, though it is not obvious, is an old picture frame. Despite the budget and materials, the house is very cozy and comfortable, being a great home for Scott.

If you are a good craftsperson, you can do this relatively easily. It will also be a fun project that can just elevate the connection you feel with your gorgeous new house. However, if you are not experienced, you can be in quite a pickle when it comes to this kind of construction. It takes only the best of the best to turn a palette into a properly insulated wall. It takes an even more impressive person to turn a few pieces of scrapped wood and plastic into functioning home elements. If you manage to do this, however, you will have achieved something amazing and something that you can be immensely proud of.

Chapter 5

Finishing Up-Things to Pay Attention To

There are often things that are overlooked at the start of construction. This can be quite damaging for your project as it will deter you when it comes to both time and finances. Of course, this is due to the nature of building a house. It is not an easy task, nor is it a simple one. It takes a lot of planning and a lot of effort. These are both commitments that a lot of us are not ready to make, so people usually have their tiny homes built for them. While it is true that leaving it to the professionals is the optimal thing to do. I mean, the people working in these companies have been doing this job for years, and it does not get much better than that. However, this, as mentioned before, can get very pricey.

Take Care of the Fragile Things

When setting up your doors and windows, make sure that you gave it as much foresight as possible. Your door should be as wide as you can make it. This will give you more natural light during the day, but it serves a much more important function. When moving things in and out of your home, you have much less space than you usually would. This means that moving around your home while holding furniture is not something you can often do. That is why a large door will help you move things around with less effort. This will also give your entrance a pleasing aesthetic, as it will feel more like home. The windows should also be large. The first reason is the same, it will let more natural light in, and it will make your house look much more spacious. They will also give your interior a much more pleasing aesthetic and will make it feel more natural as the outside will seem much closer.

Pay Attention to Aesthetics

The interior of your home is as important as the exterior. This is due to the fact that you are making a house not just to have somewhere to live, but to have somewhere you want to live in. Thus, it being pretty on the inside will be extremely important for your satisfaction with the project. If your interior looks good, you will feel better while in your home. So, is there a general rule when it comes to this? Well, not really. It is, of course, all up to taste. If you like whatever you do with your interior, that is the most important.

However, if you are not sure about what you want, there are a few guidelines that you can follow. Having a darker floor will make it look slicker. It will draw less attention from the walls and the furniture, and it will look cleaner for longer as dust and dirt are much harder to see on dark floors. This will also give you more leniency when you need to clean up. It can give you one or two more days to be lazy. The dark floors also go well with lighter tones that you might color your walls with. It will give you a good contrast of coloring and will draw more attention to the walls rather than the floors. It will also make your windows look more like they are a part of the wall rather than just an element placed there. The lighter walls will also make good use of all the natural light you are letting inside as they will make good use of the glossing. Again, these are some general guidelines. They are not something you have to follow. There is not a general rule when it comes to this, as different architectures require different aesthetics to look good. This is true for larger buildings as well, but it is far more important with tiny homes. This is due to the fact that while you look at a tiny home, you will see most of the elements that make it up. This means that playing off of the flaws of your project is very important. If you have no idea how you want to do it, you should contact an interior designer. They will probably give you the best advice you can get. If you do not want to dish out the money, however, the internet is always a place that you can visit.

You can find a lot of advice for the interior design given by people with some experience with tiny homes. Find people that have built houses similar to yours and build off of their experience, adding or removing things that you do not like. This is generally the easiest option and the most fun, as designing your interior will make it feel more intimate. You will feel as if what you made is truly yours, and that is the most important thing in a home.

Secure Your Furniture

If you are going to add furniture that is not nailed down to the floor, make sure that it is low-sitting. This means that it should be as small as possible when it comes to height. This is due to the fact that anything other than this can be potentially harmful to both you and the aesthetics of your interior. Having a lot of things that go above the waist means that you will have to watch how you are moving your arms around to avoid potentially hurting yourself. This tends to be very uncomfortable as it limits your ability to move around. Things that you have been doing your whole life can be extremely hard to do. For example, changing in and out of your clothes or anything as simple as stretching. It will also have an adverse effect on how your home looks. Tall furniture will make your small space look even smaller. It will conceal large parts of your home, making it feel more cluttered. It can also hide some of the best aspects of your home.

Sharing AND Caring

If you are living with someone else, make sure that you consider their opinion when it comes to designing and building your tiny home. I know that it might seem unnecessary to point this out, but making sure that everyone's wishes are fulfilled is extremely important with tiny homes. You will be running into your roommate very often, as there is really nowhere to go to get away from them. This means that, if tensions get high, they will probably escalate. It is already very stressful to live in a tiny home, even alone, and, until you get used to it, you might have some trouble with dealing with it. This means that you should, by all means, avoid giving anyone any reason to start a fight. If you make all of the decisions regarding the interior of your home, your roommate might feel underappreciated. After a while, this can become a running problem. You probably bought or built the home together, so it is very important to take everyone's feelings into consideration. By doing this, you can make the other person feel as if they have more of a say in the matter (which they should) and eliminates one of the potential sources of conflict. This is as important to a happy life inside of your tiny home as anything else.

When it comes to sharing your tiny home with someone, something you should always consider is your needs when it comes to privacy. If you are sharing the home with a partner that you are comfortable with, this will probably not be a problem in any way, shape, or form. However, if your roommate is someone you are not used to sharing your privacy with, you should consider the options for keeping the needs fulfilled. This is probably something you should consider as soon as possible because it can cause a lot of tension between you.

Handling Pets

For the more tiny roommates of the furry kind, there are a few things to think about as well. If you have a dog or cat and you want to give them the ability to enter your home and exit it at will, you should install a pet door as well. It will take a great deal of retraining as well because you do not have enough room for the facilities required for a pet. Fortunately, your backyard is large enough to host them. If your pet is used to living inside, it might be difficult to get them to spend their time outside. However, this will be very beneficial for both you and your pet. It is not a secret that outside doing wonders for pets. It is healthy for them and will keep them happy. Of course, your pet being outside will also motivate you to do so as well. This is extremely good for your health as well, and it serves a great recreational purpose. Living inside of a tiny home can often feel very constricting, and going outside to let out some steam will do wonders for you. Cats and dogs are simple enough to deal with, but other pets might be a bit more problematic. For example, fish, hamsters, and birds might be quite difficult to manage with the limited space. A cage or aquarium can take up a lot of space, and it just might be some space that you need for something. I do not recommend getting animals like this unless you are ready to spend a pretty penny.

Cages and aquariums can be built into your furniture. Crazy constructions like this have been a thing of fashion for a very long time. While it's true there's a lot of TV shows that feature this kind of contraption, they are, of course, expensive. But having a cage built into your cupboard or an aquarium that doubles as a table will both look cool and give you animal companionship without deteriorating any of your other plans. An outdoor aquarium isn't the smartest thing ever. Too many things can go wrong due to how fragile the glass can be. There are a lot of other elements that can easily break due to the elements.

Stray cats and dogs can also cause quite a problem. Birds, on the other hand, are another story. You can build an outdoor birdhouse, but this might be an easy way to lose your pet due to them flying away. Of course, you can always train your pet in order not to do so, but this might be extremely difficult without a professional. However, having a "public" birdhouse can be very relaxing due to the lack of responsibility. It is a recreational task, at worst. You can just pop out whenever you want and toss around some bird food and enjoy the chirping. If you are more attached to your pets, you can always build an outdoor birdcage. This is a bit complicated and takes quite a bit of money and effort. You are going to have to have an incredible amount of insulation and ways to defend from the elements. It would also have to be incredibly sturdy due to strong winds. While this can be very difficult, it will be an amazing addition to your yard. It will be amazing to look at.

Ensure Your Financing's Secure

Make sure that you are financially able to hold your own inside of your tiny home. As you might know, owning any kind of house comes with a lot of costs. In regular houses, this can be somewhat subverted by renting out parts of it. In a tiny home, this is not an option. If your tiny home isn't something that you planned to share with someone, you should not even attempt it. You will probably never find someone that wants to rent a section of a single room and, if you do, it is going to be quite a task to get used to living with them. This person will usually not have the same goals or plans as you. They might not even be ready to do everything that is required to efficiently live in a tiny home, especially with someone else.

The problem arises if they are not the pinnacle of reason, as it is hard to negotiate the conditions and limitations of this deal. You might be ready to give up most of your things that are not necessary, but they might not. It is hard to get people to give up things they are fond of if it is not originally of their own volition.

Another difficulty may arise when talking about responsibilities. Though the home is extremely small, there are things that need to be done, and a lot of them are not easy. Privacy might also be a problem, especially if they are not ready to give up some of it. Make sure that they are aware of what needs to be done and what they need to get used to. Even then, if they are willing to make all of these changes, adjusting to living with someone will be difficult, especially due to the spatial limitations. It tends to be very unnerving to share your life in such a way with anyone, especially a stranger. However, going through these difficulties with someone might help you become close to them. Getting a friend that can go through such difficulties with you will be a very valuable addition to your life.

Test Your Construction

Before moving into your home, make sure that it is safe to move into. While the construction might seem stable and strong at first glance, there are many things that you might not have foreseen. Oversights are not a rarity when it comes to this either. This is because you just do not know if you have made a mistake before you experience problems. This is why you should have a professional at hand as much as possible. Even a consultation upon finishing the project can go a long way when it comes to the safety of your new building. If you do not make sure that it is a hundred percent safe, many things can go poorly. Your roof can get blown off. Your walls can last much shorter than they should if you do not properly cover them. You can have problems when it comes to heating up your home if you do not do a proper job with your insulation. Natural occurrences like winds and small earthquakes can destroy your home if the construction isn't excellently made. There are just too many things that can go wrong, so you should not risk it. Make sure that your new home is home, safe, and sound.

Heating is something that you need to pay attention to as well. Again, you have plenty of options for this; however, you need to be very informed to do this properly. Different environments require different kinds of heating. The unpredictability of how air behaves in tiny spaces just adds to the puzzle. This turns the task into a thing of trial and error. You are going to need a lot of time to find something that is just right for you. There are a lot of people who talk about this online. Again, if you want to cut down the cost and time requirement, you should always turn to threads spread all over the internet for advice. While your home will most definitely be unique, you can find people who have similar ones. You can learn a lot from their experiences. This will also give you some peace of mind as you know that your solution has worked perfectly for someone before.

Upon finishing your construction, you need to be ready to add superfluous amounts of hooks and shelves. This is the best way for you to save as much space as possible. A lot of shelves will keep your items relatively properly sorted. It will also keep it from getting in your way while you perform your every-day tasks. The more shelves you manage to hammer into your walls, the more things from your old life you get to keep. This helps alleviate the pressure you feel to throw away things and lets you know where everything is even in the most chaotic of situations. The hooks are useful for storing additional clothes. You will probably not be able to spare the space for a cabinet where you can store your clothes. Placing hooks over places where you will not walk like above your bed will help you store your additional clothes in such a way that they will not take up any space that you might use for something more important.

Depending on where you are building your home, you should research the laws that govern construction there. We are not just talking about the land and the permits that you need for the house and moving it. In certain countries of the world, you need special permits to add things like solar panels to your home. It is very important to stay informed when it comes to this and make sure that you get all of the permits cleaned up as soon as possible.

Chapter 6

Living in a Tiny Home

Living in a tiny home might seem much cheaper than a regular home. However, this might be untrue. People often overlook a number of additional expenses. While it is true that a hundred thousand dollars for a home is less than several hundred thousand dollars, the problems arise in other areas. The problem with land is prominent in every construction project; it comes with a few twists with tiny homes.

This is especially true when it comes to mobile homes, as renting land is a whole new different story. If you are looking to throw yourself into a project like that, you should research the laws that account for your case. It can often be problematic to work out prices for additional work to make upgrades to your house. They can often be more expensive than in regular-sized homes. It is a small and fragile construction, so it is much harder to work around it. Changing your interior can also be a huge issue. Moving large things in and out of your home is hell, especially considering how limited your space is when you account for the fact that there are going to be a lot of items inside of it once you start moving things around.

Tiny homes can also be incredibly pricey to maintain. It is true that you will need fewer repairs and that they will mostly be much smaller than usual, the fragile construction of your small house will make it harder to do the heavy-duty maintenance and repairs that most buildings do. On top of this, moving your home might be a problem due to the costs of towing equipment. Before committing to a tiny house, you should put in work to research how much you are going to break your bank.

The main upsides of owning a tiny house are the relative cheapness and greenness that comes with it. These are some adjectives that are easy to throw around but hard to live by. If it is truly your goal to make them into your own golden rules, there is a huge journey of changing your lifestyle in front of you. For starters, tiny homes come with a vast array of different problems that can be solved in numerous ways. While some are less expensive and more eco-friendly than others, they are less pretty too. Though living in the 21st century comes with its own commodities, you will have to give some of them up. For example, you will not be able to have the big bathroom that you usually would in a regular house. This is a huge deal-breaker for a lot of people, as personal hygiene is a thing a lot of us are squeamish about. We got so used to the commodities offered to us by large homes that we do not consider them commodities at all anymore. Well, living in a tiny home will remind you of that fact.

Tiny homes are illegal in some places as well. Well, not really illegal. There isn't a specific ban placed on them. However, you will not be able to place your mobile tiny home everywhere. Finding a zone where you might be able to live might be problematic, so you should get into that as soon as possible.

There are also a few things you should get used to when it comes to functioning within the limits of your house. First, remember that most of your furniture will be built in. This means that you will have to consider your placement while it is being built and make peace with it. Also, know that everything in your home should be, or rather, has to be multipurpose. Your staircase becomes a storage area. Your counter doubles as your bed. Your entire bathroom is your shower, and your kitchen cupboards double as your cabinet. Everything has several purposes. This might be hard to get used to, but it will take you no more than a few days to do so.

Planning Ahead

Foresight is extremely important. You can't just say you are going to buy a home with a random set of furniture. If you are not used to a minimalist lifestyle, you need to pick out what kind of uses you want from your items. When you buy a pre-made home, you won't be able to replace the heavy-duty furniture. There are just so many things you need to consider. Medical conditions, physical weaknesses, pets, your height, etc. Be very careful and meticulous when you try to figure out what works best for you.

Climate is also a huge factor. It is relatively easy to insulate a huge house, or rather, it has better baseline insulation. While your home can easily be insulated, you should consider the climate of your surroundings before you find your home. Places with extreme heat or cold can be problematic to live in a tiny home. Being locked inside a tiny space in the scorching sun is not pleasant. Neither is living in the chilling cold in a badly insulated space. Make sure that your location is fitting for your intentions with your tiny home. The elements can take quite a toll on even the strongest constructions, and the same, if not more, can be said for something like this.

Moving in might prove to be quite difficult as well. This is due to the fact that it is a whole other story than regular moving. Your family and friends will probably not have any experience with this. On top of that, it takes a great deal of foresight to do it properly. While moving, there are many other elements to take into consideration. When buying any new home, timing is very important. Even though the trend of tiny homes has been present for decades, you will rarely find anyone selling their tiny home property. This means that you will often have to build it from the ground up. This will prove to be a difficult endeavor during winter. Putting on the finishing touches will be a problem in harsh colds as well. Even when you are looking to order a premade tiny home, know that harsh weather will impact your delivery time. There are a few other things that you should consider. If you have children in the household, make sure to move at the end of the school year. Keep your health in check. While moving is always a physically challenging task, the greater difficulty comes with mental health. Make sure that you are at your best when you start the project. Buying a house is always very stressful. That much is especially true with tiny homes as there are so many difficulties you might face. It is not easy to get used to the minimalist lifestyle. It might quickly take its toll on you, and if you aren't at your best, you might be in some big trouble. Big decisions like this are always hard to make, so take your time if you can.

Check Out Legalities

There are quite a few difficulties with living in tiny homes. We mentioned the placement problem before. There are several zones where parking your mobile tiny home is illegal. If you are building a tiny home from the ground up, you should check this upfront. Why? Because it might get awkward when you find that your town's law doesn't take too kindly to your project. Luckily for you, you can find guides all over the internet. People have already done the research, and all you need to do is read up on it.

One of the upsides of living in a larger house is that with many rooms divided by walls is the fact that you can have privacy whenever you want. When it comes to self-care, having a little bit of peace and quiet can go a long way. It can actually be the key to a happy life. However, with tiny houses, this is a luxury that you do not have. The privacy factor will not be a problem only within the household, but also outside of it. While tiny homes have been present for a relatively long time, they are still a novelty as not many people live in them. What this means is that you will get strange looks and people that want to see how it looks. Having large windows in small rooms leaves the house open to peering eyes from the outside. It is hard to keep up your daily routine with the thought of it being almost public. While yes, you will have the support of your family, this, too, is a double-edged sword. By that, I mean that something that seems so small, so insignificant, can cause huge ructions. No matter how small the problem is, it has the chance to cause a chain reaction within the family.

This is especially true if you are trapped within a small space for the majority of the day. People often miss the ability to isolate themselves in another room for some me-time. There are, however, ways to fix these issues. As with regular houses, you can install some shades to protect your privacy from the outside world. This also helps keep your home a bit cooler when the summer heats start hitting your town.

While protecting your privacy from the peering eyes of your neighbors is relatively easy, the real issues lie inside of the house. You can, however, turn the problem around and make it into a fun game. Finding creative solutions to divide up space can be pretty fun. Again, you can use shades inside of your house to use them as pseudo-walls to assure some privacy. Alternatively, you can use the alignment of your furniture to set up a safe space for yourself. Also, you should remember that you are not tied down to the interior of your house. The best part of living in a tiny home is that the world around you is just an extension of the place you call home. You can always find a nice space under a tree, in the grass, and set up a makeshift bed or set up a hammock between two trees. The tiny home lifestyle is all about living freely and not being tied down to your house.

It is true that the maintenance costs of tiny homes are much smaller than with regular houses. This is one of the best things about them. People often use this as the main reason for opting for a tiny home rather than a bigger one. However, these houses are quite unpredictable. For example, heating will always be an issue. Not because it is harder to cover the space, but because tiny homes hold heat much different to how most of us are used to. Keeping your home cool can be very easy. You just open up a few windows, and the temperature drops easily. Heating up your home is a whole different game. It is hard to predict how the tiny space is going to conduct heat, and you might have to go through a lot of trial and error.

This problem is relatively easy to fix. Centralized heating is the best solution, of course, but installing it can be quite problematic and pricey. Maintaining it isn't the easiest either. It also goes against the eco-friendliness of the tiny home model. There are plenty of options for the greener of us. You can install smaller heating units that run on green energy. This is a great option, though a bit pricey.

However, you can always consider this an investment. This kind of heating will be very cost-efficient over longer periods of time. On top of that, this will take up less space. The space they can take up is almost ignorable, even though your house might not be the biggest. Wireless thermostats are an option too. They are easy to use, and you can use them on your mobile phone. This means that you can heat up your home from a distance, so you are welcomed with a warm and cozy atmosphere after a long day at work. Isn't it great?

Be it as it may, it is extremely important to take heating into consideration when building your home.

Bid Goodbye to Unnecessary Things

People have difficulties with storing items in tiny homes. It is hard to give up some of your things, but any kind of unnecessary luggage can be too much for your tiny space. You can't find an empty corner, because it is usually something that you do not have. Thus, people that are not used to the minimalist lifestyle often try to find new solutions for storing goods. These solutions come with additional costs. Renting a storage unit is an obvious choice. However, this goes directly against the tiny home lifestyle. If you opt to build a tiny home, you aim for lower costs of living and, when renting a storage unit, the cost is just going to keep racking up as it isn't exactly the cheapest thing ever. This, of course, is not your only option. You can always find a friend that has room to spare. If you are not willing to dish out the cash, this is a good solution for temporary storage. Another thing you can do is build/buy a shed. As mentioned before, tiny homes often have huge backyards that have a lot of unused space. Luckily you can use this space to make your own storage unit. However, this is not recommended if you have a lot of fragile items that are sensitive to the elements. Of course, that is if you do not plan to make your shed a piece of state of the art construction.

A lot of people buy groceries in bulk to save a lot of money. You will not have this option, however. That is due to the limited spacing. To be more accurate, your tiny home will often have a tiny fridge. This means that you will have to find alternative ways to get your hands on cheap groceries. You can always look into local ads to find dirt-cheap groceries. Other than that, you can find a farmers' market in your local area. If that kind of thing is not available to you, you can buy from smaller stores as they often offer better deals. If you insist on buying in bulk, you can get a larger fridge or freezer that you can place outside of your house. By doing so, you can keep your groceries unspoiled as you would with a large house.

Be Wary Of Clutter

As mentioned before, cluttering your already limited space can be a problem. This kind of space can only work if it is clean. You really cannot afford the space that a pile of clothes takes up on the floor. The weight of your interior can come into play when transporting your home elsewhere. As the basic elements of the house are relatively heavy, each pound of additional weight can kill your moving plan. It might seem easy to clean up after yourself in such a small space; it might prove challenging. You need to be a perfectionist at all times. There is no room for laziness. The best thing you can do to make for more storage inside your home is to use your furniture as storage areas. You can keep some clothes under the pillows of your couch or under the mattress of your bed. The options are many, but not infinite. Another option to keep your floor uncluttered is using the walls. It is relatively easy to build in movable cubes inside of your walls and floor. This is both very efficient and helps you feel like your home is a unique creation. In big houses, you can also let your clutter stay for one or two days, but not in tiny homes. You can always build in floor vents that double as sweepers.

Work with What You've Got

With tiny homes, garbage disposal can also be a big issue. You do not have the traditional options that you usually do. This is because trash disposal services usually come around weekly or bi-weekly. However, you have some options that can help you out with this. The first thing that every household, not only tiny ones, should start doing is gathering things into compost. This can make some very healthy mulch that you can use to rejuvenate the plant life around your home. It is also useful if you like natural decoration. Planting flowers is both a good hobby and a great way to decorate your tiny home and give it a new glow. Other than that, it can help you reduce your cost by helping you grow your own fruits and vegetables. This is healthy for the environment, and it is a good thing to do on a regular basis. Other than this, you can deliver your garbage directly to the land-fill. This will pull you back when it comes to gas money, but it is a good way to get rid of your trash bags. While it is impossible to live trash free, you can always cut down on your trash production by switching to reusable items like mugs and bags. Using glass containers instead of plastic will also increase the time your groceries are usable before spoiling.

Buying things is a new challenge, all on its own. Why? While working with limited space, you need to think about the place of every item you might pick up. You always have to ask yourself if it is truly necessary to purchase the item. If you come to the conclusion that it isn't, but you still want it, you need to figure out if you can afford the space for it. If not, but you still really want it, you need to find something to remove from your household. While I know that one little souvenir from a trip might seem like nothing, it will prove to be a lot. If you start making exceptions, you will start to make them more and more often. What this means, in return, is that your tiny home just keeps becoming tinier. The same and more is true for mobile homes. Not only the size but also the weight comes into play in these situations. While yes, I am sure a gorgeous kitchen counter will look amazing inside that tiny space, can you really risk the hazards that come with it? The potential hazards are many. Being heavy, it can easily break whatever it is on during transportation, meaning that a lot of your valuables get destroyed. It is also a question of piled up weight. No vehicle in the world has an infinite carrying capacity. On top of all of that, anything large will be very difficult to both put inside of your home and then take it out. You just do not have enough space to make errors, and the potential to make them is always there.

And when it comes to the happenings of your day to day life, clutter is a big problem. A few shirts and wrappers here and there might not make much a change in regular homes. Here, however, they do.

One spilled bowl of cereal can spell disaster for your floor. You always need to be vigilant in cleaning up behind yourself. If you don't, the clutter will get overwhelming. This is not catastrophic from a physical standpoint as the worst-case scenario is that you need to spend one whole day just cleaning up. The mental strain of having a messy tiny home can be quite something, on the other hand. This is especially true if you are new to the whole gig. You are probably already stressed out during your first few weeks. It is a lot to take in and get used to, and any bit of clutter, no matter how small, looks huge in relation to the size of your home. It is really easy to get stressed out at the sight of even the simplest of problems when you find yourself in a new environment.

All of this can often be discouraging. After all, it is a very big change and hard to get used to. However, perseverance is the key. You need to be ready for a lot of trial and error. There really isn't a guide that will tell you everything you need to do. It is a journey of discovery that you need to embark on. It is up to you and nobody else to discover what works and what does not. Every family has their own needs and wants, which are rarely the same as another's, so it is almost always hard to figure out what works best. Just keep trying, and you will get there.

The first few weeks will be the most difficult. There are a lot of adjustments to be made; however, in time, you will find a rhythm that works for you.

If you do persevere, however, and you find yourself inside of your home, you get a rare chance in life that not many people do. While yes, there are downsides to this kind of lifestyle, and I have mentioned a lot of the above, there are just so many positives that make it worth the trouble.

Something that can never be stressed enough is how cheap a tiny house is going to be. While professionally built ones can cost tens of thousands of dollars, DIY houses will usually cost no more than 30,000 US dollars. It is amazing how big the difference is, with your average large house costing a few hundred thousand. Of course, you will feel the difference in size in other areas as well. Your water and electricity bills will be much lower. As you are working with a smaller space, there are fewer things to help you stack them up. While maintenance can be a bit more stressful than in your average home, it will almost always be much cheaper.

The sinker for most people, when it comes to tiny homes, is the mortgage part of the deal. Well, to be more accurate, the lack of it. To build or buy a regular home, a lot of people need to take up mortgages. We all know what kind of a burden this is. We have seen it on TV and in real life numerous times. While a mortgage might seem like a good thing sometimes, it never is. Like any other form of debt, it just keeps piling up. It is life-draining to live with. The constant stress of knowing that something you worked so hard for can be taken away in a short matter of time can be devastating. Mortgages will just drain you, both mentally and financially. And by the time you pay it off (if you do), you will not feel like you have won anything. You just lost a huge amount of money over a long period of time, but this is usually not a problem with tiny homes. Portable tiny homes do not need any kind of additional investment when it comes to the construction itself. Tiny homes with foundations, on the other hand, require land. But this is much more manageable than dishing out a few hundred thousand on the building itself and then another hundred thousand on the land needed. Tiny homes give you the chance to live your life mortgage-free. Nobody can tell you how valuable that is then people that actually have mortgages. This helps you fund your retirement plans, trips, etc. All in all, having that little bit of money that you wouldn't have any other way will improve your life by quite a bit.

With the smaller size also comes smaller energy consumption. While, yes, this comes back to cost less to heat up or power your house, it also serves to minimize your footprint. A single wooden stove is usually enough to heat up an entire tiny house. On top of that, living off the grid is much easier in a tiny home due to that too. If you want to live a life independent of as many things as possible, portable tiny homes will give you just that.

Another thing that portable tiny homes give you is the amazing freedom of movement. Being on the road means a lot of the same for most people. People always assume that it is uncomfortable and that you need to give up the home you are used to. They see it as a drastic change of environment etc. If you manage to turn your living quarters into a vehicle, being on the road has never been easier. We talked about houses being built on trailers before. This comes with some incredible upsides. You will always feel at home on the road because you always are. People underestimate how valuable that is when it comes to long trips. Being away from home for months can be very difficult for some, especially if it is something that they have dedicated a great deal of time and effort to build and maintain. For a lot of people, this is the preferred way of traveling.

People like to think that by living in a smaller home makes them closer to nature. To be honest, I can't agree more. Think about it.

Imagine that you had some land. You can build a big home on it and have a small backyard. This will be fulfilling for a very short time, as the wow factor dissipates very quickly. After that, you are left with hefty maintenance bills and a lot of space that needs to be cleaned. Quite frankly, the space you are burning all that money into is probably not even used that well. What I am getting at is that behind all of that luxury and conformity, it ends up being extremely shallow and a huge burden. Now let's say that you have the same piece of land, but this time, you want to place a tiny home on it. What does this mean? Well, for starters, you leave nature much more room to flourish. I mean, isn't it obvious. The less of the land you use actually to build things, the more green is left untouched. This gives your home a sort of Eden-like feeling, where you can go out in the morning, sit on a rock, and watch how the world around you is just brimming with life. While you might love a big home, you will enjoy a huge green area even more. Having so much free space has its benefits as well. You always wanted a garden? Well, that's nice, now you can have one. Wanted a dog? Check. Need a lot of room so that you can organize a huge BBQ? You got it. There are just so many benefits to large yards. And believe me, they are a luxury. When buying a regular house, if you also want a huge yard, you will have to dish out a pretty penny.

On the subject of staying green, the size of your new home will also help you be more eco-friendly. Solar panels are an incredible invention. They can help us secure the lifestyle that we are used to without dealing with Mother Nature any more blows than we already have. However, powering a large house through solar panels can be incredibly taxing. It comes with some steep costs for both installation and maintenance. With a tiny home, you will rarely need more than one solar panel.

Another thing that goes to show the openness of tiny homes that you can do is use the outside of your home as a part of the interior. What does this mean? For example, you can put some furniture outside. Using a small space outside of your home as a dining room is a good way to save some room. By setting up a smaller construction with a few beams and some nail-ons, you can make a makeshift terrace that you can use for your meals. There is nothing bad about eating outside. Rather, it is preferable. Having a nice lunch while surrounded by all of the lush greenness of mother nature is extremely pleasant. Another thing you can do is line one wall with water-proof dressers to have some more storage area. Alternatively, you can always keep your freezer outside of your house to save up some more space.

The minimalist lifestyle required to flourish in a tiny home also requires you to make some sacrifices. I do not mean this in a bad way. It is just that tiny homes have a way of making you be more eco-friendly no matter what. For example, there is a larger urgency to dispose of trash as soon as possible. This, in turn, motivates you to start composting. This is not only good for the environment but can help you with any personal projects that you might take part of in the future. The lifestyle is greener by default. You use materials that are less harmful to your surroundings and at a lower quantity right off the bat.

On top of that, the building process is extremely intimate with small houses. While yes, there have been cases of people building a regular-sized home from scratch on their own, this will take months, if not years. With a tiny house, you will remember every nail you hammered and every board in the process. It will truly be something that you love and nurture. Even after construction is done, the intimacy you will have with your creation will be irreplaceable. While, yes, it can be tiring to look at the same thing over and over again, bonding with a home has never been easier. There is less of it to bond with. However, what little there is has a lot of character. It is easy to love, despite the difficulties. It is true that downsizing and getting rid of your beloved items is hard. Whenever you get something new, you will know that that something is really special and has a special place in your house, and not only your heart. It is what a home should be, a place that you know by heart.

Another thing that attracts people is the simple lifestyle; it not only encourages but makes it necessary. It is hard to get used to. If it is something you are not ready for, I suggest waiting a bit before opting for a tiny home. However, if you are ready for it, you will find it to be rewarding beyond all measure. Living a lifestyle where you suppress your materialism is hard when the only downside is that you are spending money on things. It is not as simple when you are working with 200 square feet of floor space. It discourages materialism as much as humanly possible. Fancy electronics, books, clothes, decorations are all a burden when you live in such a small space. The tiny home lifestyle requires you to cut down all of your needs right to the essentials and nothing more. It gives room for sentiment, of course, just not much. This can be a huge turning point for a lot of people as, with the temptations of the 21st century, it is hard to live a life of only the basics. But if you manage to do so, it will be a cathartic experience. It is just so simple once you get used to it.

When on auto-pilot, you just have fewer things to think about and worry about. The one plant you have in that one corner that you keep looking at will become a good friend to you. As your responsibilities grow fever, they start meaning more to you on a personal level. If the necessary time to perform them all drops from an hour to fifteen minutes, you get the chance to actually take your time and enjoy watering your plant or feeding your dog. Changing your sheets stops being a mundane task. Rather it becomes something that you enjoy as, without a lot of room, it is one of the few things that you can switch up inside of your house. Everything just means so much more. This comes back to the intimacy mentioned above. You won't feel like you are living in just any other small house. It can truly become your home. It might be just 200 square feet, but it is the 200 square feet you feel homesick about when you are away. Alternatively, they are the 200 square feet that follow you everywhere you go and that you can rely on for everything. A tiny home is just so much easier to love. I believe that this is due to the social aspect of house owning.

People expect a successful working person to own a home, and the size of the home often reflects the size of the success. Thus we are forced into this ridiculous game of comparing each other based on the sizes of our homes. Home became an expectation. You can look at tiny homes as a way to take the purity of what a home is back. It becomes a choice again. It becomes something that you want and works for of your own accord.

Chapter 7

Tips and Tricks

You will have to get used to an extremely minimalist lifestyle if you are to live in a tiny home. This lifestyle is not for hoarders or messy people. You can't afford the space that random rubbish makes on your floor. Anything that is not essential or multipurpose has to go. If your decorations don't double as storage, don't keep it. On top of that, clothes and random items that you might want to keep also need to go if you do not have a way of efficiently storing them. You need to figure out in advance what your home can take. On top of that, keep one rule in mind. "Whenever you buy something, you have to get rid of something else." This might seem hard to get used to, but once you do, it will become second nature. It will also make your life easier. Shopping sprees will cost you much less. Decorating and cleaning up will never be a problem as you have much less to decorate or clean. On top of that, your home will always have an incredibly warm feel as you will have a deep connection with all of the items in your house. Every shelf, pillow, and lamp will be a close friend. You will see them often and use them often. This kind of lifestyle is the definition of "It's not much, but it's honest work."

If you live with someone else, especially if it is more than one person, you should set up a schedule. Not just when it comes to using the bathroom. I am talking about absolutely anything that you might argue over. Living in a tiny home with someone else in a tiny home can be very stressful. You will always be looking at them, running into them, and sharing the same space for most things. It is easy to get into a fight over such a thing. It will be very strenuous, as you might imagine. Thus, to avoid unnecessary conflict, you should set up schedules for everything you can. When you are reading, you usually do not want anyone around you. You really need the peace and quiet to focus on whatever you might be interested in. To avoid fights with your family, partner, or friends, you should come to an agreement over who can use which facilities when. If you have hobbies that take up a bit of space, you should talk about a timetable that works for everyone in the household. This might be relatively hard to adjust to, but then again, moving into a tiny home is just a series of difficult adjustments.

When decorating, you are going to have to hold back a little bit. I know that you want your house to be your little paradise and that there are a lot of things you want to add to it. However, ask yourself if it is worth space. We have discussed at length how everything in your house needs to have a practical function. That being said, if you really want to decorate your home, here are a few tips. Use your exterior as much as possible. Of course, this goes much further than just paint. There are a lot of ways you can decorate your exterior. Gardening is always a nice hobby to have. Other than that, if you get good at it and manage to maintain a pretty garden, it will give a lot of character to your little home. It is no secret that this makes any home prettier. It is especially true for small homes. In larger houses, flowers work on decorating parts of the construction to make it lighter on the eyes. When it comes to small constructions, flowers work more towards making the house pop and stand out. Due to the small size, it is easy to absorb the whole sight from just one angle, and that is why flowers round out the appearance. It will make it look more natural as well like it was always meant to be there. Other than flowers, a padded path surrounded by a tiny fence or little statues will give your little house a lot of character. A large backyard (which is very common with tiny homes) will give you a lot of opportunities to make your yard extremely unique. Your imagination is the limit, to be honest.

While we are talking about exterior design, it is important to mention the fact that having a big and empty backyard can be very unsightly. Your house will always be the star of the show, but having a huge space around your home will make a show of its flaws. Every single bit of mis-colored wall or dirty wood will be obvious to see. On top of that, the space on its own will not be easy on the eyes. So, to summarize, make sure to use the space in your yard as efficiently as on the inside. The good news is the fact that all of this gives you a lot of freedom when it comes to decorations. It is always good to use the ground you have for flowers and the like. Alternatively, having a vegetable garden or a lot of fruit trees will both look good and have a lot of functional use. It will give you something to do with your compost. It will make your day to day life cheaper because you are getting food from your own home. It will also go toward making your home look more natural.

When we talk about interior decorations, there are a few options, though they are limited. Of course you can go for a huge chandelier, but that just won't do. It might be a part of your grand vision, but let's be real, you cannot spare enough room for that. Luckily there are many smaller alternatives. You can go to smaller chandeliers. This will free up some room for you as well as give your home a modern look. Building your lighting into your ceiling is an option. It is something that is done very often in big houses. This is a bit inefficient as you will need more light sources to provide enough lighting, but it will give your ceiling a very slick look. This option will also save you the most space as you are using space that was already used for something else just as you should with as many things as you can. The best way you can customize your interior is by using things that can be hung on walls. Mirrors, as mentioned before, will make your rooms look much wider than they actually are. They will also work towards giving different angles for looking at the interior from one spot, which is always great when you want to show off your taste.

When you are looking towards saving the last bits of storage space you want, you can, though I do not recommend it, start using plastic plates. Alternatively, you can, as mentioned before, store your excess plates and dishes outside of your home, especially if they are ceramic, as they can endure a bit more exposure to the elements. However, plastic plates are much easier to store, though they are much less eco-friendly. They are also much easier to transport, as you do not have to worry that they will break, and even if they get damaged, the cost of replacing them will be much lower. However, this will also probably increase the amount of trash your produce over time, so take that into consideration as well.

While we are on the subject of waste production, there are many kinds of plumbing you can go for if you are building on the land. In an RV, you have a single option, though. If you do not fancy going to a gas station whenever you need to take care of your needs, a waste tank is necessary. While building on foundations, however, you have a plethora of options that vary in cost and function. You can always go for regular plumbing. This has worked for as long as it existed; however, we all know that it is not exactly eco-friendly. On the other hand, composting bathrooms and septic tanks are options. A septic tank is the cheapest to build and the easiest to maintain. However, waste disposal can be very messy, and it is not for the squeamish. It is not exactly the most hygienic solution either, nor is it very eco-friendly. A composting bathroom is as the name suggests. Bathrooms that turn your waste into compost. This, again, is not exactly the most hygienic thing ever. However, it is an incredibly good way to handle your waste disposal. It is very healthy for the environment, not only for the fact that it can be used to help plants grow but also for the fact that the final point of the waste does not damage any animal life. Regular plumbing, as well as septic tanks, are usually emptied into some large body of water. This has a huge impact on the plant and animal life that inhabits it. Mostly in a bad way, as feces are, as you may imagine, very damaging to fish and the like.

Waste gathered in composting bathrooms, on the other hand, ends up in the ground, helping plant life grow. You can use this compost to help your garden if you have one. This is yet another reason to have lush plant life around your home as it gives you an efficient use for your compost. This brings you closer to sustaining yourself at as little of a cost as possible. This will save you a little bit of money, as well as time you might need to spend grocery shopping. This will also help you feel like your own person, helping the land so that it can help you. Another option you have when it comes to your waste disposal is incineration. Incinerator toilets are relatively new on the market and are rarely used outside of tiny homes. They are not too expensive, but they will save you a lot of effort. They are often seen on yachts or RVs. Be it as it may, it is a relatively eco-friendly way of feces disposal. Instead of wasting water, these toilets burn feces and turn them into pathogen-free ash. Similarly to compost toilets, this will prevent your feces from damaging aquatic ecosystems; however, it does increase your carbon footprint. It also saves you a lot of time and resources as it disposes of your waste on its own. On top of that, it is very hygienic. It is a very niche option, but it is one that is available to you and is not bad. The best thing is that it can be powered by any kind of energy including, but not limited to, gas, electricity, and even dried feces. Incineration toilets are very efficient and fast, so if that is what you are looking for, go for this option.

Having people over can be quite a problem too, especially if you want to entertain a large group. The lack of space just becomes worse than ever, especially considering the fact that the people coming over won't be used to the tiny home lifestyle. On top of that, you won't be used to working around so many people in your house. That is why it is smart to have an outdoor set-up. A few folding chairs or stools, as well as a foldable table, will work wonders. With a decent yard, you don't have to worry about your guests being cramped up in a tiny space. The foldable furniture will also take up very little space; at the end of the day, that is why they were designed the way they are.

Even if you do not have guests often, having some foldable furniture will do wonders for you. During mild spring days, you can go outside, enjoy the weather, read a book or crack open a cold beer and just relax on your foldable chair. Foldables are also a great addition to any camping trip or BBQ. You won't regret having one or two of these at your disposal, as they are a great way to save space in your house, folding your chair after having a nice meal to make room so that you can do some yoga or anything of the sort.

If you have a regular table with a large tablecloth, you get another way of saving space. You can use this opportunity to store some things below your table. Stacking up a few boxes of clothes or books can not only save you space but also give a wobbly table some stability. You can do the same with your other furniture. As mentioned before, putting clothes under the pillows of your couch also works. If you build tall enough and stable enough, you might even get an attic-like space. This is not easy to do, especially on your own, so I suggest getting the help of a professional if you are concerned with keeping as many of your belongings as possible.

Conclusion

A tiny home is something unique, to be certain. It is not just a thing of size. It just has a unique charm to it that cannot be denied or ignored. While having a huge house is something that has been presented to us as a badge of success for centuries, times are changing. The societal norm has changed in such a way where the worth of a person became a thing of more than one factor. While money is important, our horizons have expanded exponentially. Everything that has gone down in the past few decades has relatively quickly changed the way we look at the world. Especially now, when individualism has become more important than ever. While running after a huge house to prove your economic ability to both yourself and others is nothing to scoff at, it is not the only thing that we can do. Wanting a large home is fairly respectable. It is an individualistic choice that any single one of us can make, and there is nothing wrong with making it. To some people, bigger is always better, and that is completely fine. However, many of us do not see the world like that. The societal pressure placed on us to build larger can be quite suffocating, and it just inspires us to go against it. That is why tiny homes are so unique.

Building a tiny home sends a message. By doing so, you are telling the world that you are not tied down to traditional materialism. The gleam of living in a palace does not appeal to you, and you just want to live a comfortable and contained life. Another thing it says about you is that you are not afraid to explore new frontiers. While it is true that tiny homes have been a thing for more than two decades, they are still relatively new. The percentage of homeowners that live inside of tiny homes is still very small. Yet, this does not scare you. Rather, knowing what lies ahead, the benefits, and the challenges, only make the prospect more exciting. You want your home to be your own. You want to know what is in each corner by heart, and you want to be intimately connected to everything inside and outside of it. You are not afraid of building it alone; rather, it just becomes more special to you because you built it with your own hands. There is a thing of spiritualism that can be found here. While you do not feel completely free yourself from conformism, you are slowly letting go of it to live a simpler and more pure lifestyle. A lifestyle that is not for anyone, of course. While it is difficult to get used to, this lifestyle is as rewarding as life gets. It is all about discarding what is unnecessary and keeping that which makes you the happiest.

Of course, money is always a factor when it comes to making a living. If you do not have hundreds of thousands of dollars to dish out on the house, you are in luck. A tiny house costs far less than a regular one by a margin of several times. To buy or build a regular house, you will most often need a mortgage. They say that this is the best way to get yourself in debt for life. This is, unfortunately, often true, as a lot of people take decades to pay off their mortgages, often sacrificing luxuries that could have made them happier during their lives. If you do not mind not going on yearly trips to exotic locations and putting far less money than you should into your pension fund, by all means, go for it. However, most people fear mortgages, deeming them to be the greatest evil brought to us by capitalism, with good reason too. In many third-world and even second-world countries, mortgages are known to go as far as even ruining lives. Though you might not be in the position where such a thing can happen to you, a mortgage can put a hefty amount of pressure on you, both financially and mentally. As you might imagine, you will be paying far more money than you got from the deal, and this might slow down whatever plans you have for the future. It is also very stressful, even if your budget does not feel the difference.

The fact that it is something hanging over your head and that can cause you a lot of trouble with just one unfortunate event. It is quite sad; frankly, that wanting an idyllic family life can place you in such a problem. A tiny home, while not ideal for making a family, is the cheapest and closest alternative. While it is true that a good bunch of tiny homes can cost a bit over 100,000 US dollars, there are much cheaper alternatives. However, even the most expensive options will cost less than a full-sized house. Even if you need a mortgage to build a tiny home, it will be much easier to pay off as the amount of money is not as substantial.

Another comparison can be made when we are talking about building a home yourself. While it is not rare for people to build their own full-sized houses to cut down the costs, this takes months and sometimes even years. Obviously, a tiny home would take much less time to build. However, the difference in the time elapsed is huge. Incredibly, a tiny home can be built in a matter of weeks. This is no exaggeration. If you can hire a crew of people, this becomes much less, but a lot of people reported building their homes in as little time as ten weeks. On top of that, designing a tiny home is much easier too. While the difficulty of working with less space can be felt, it makes things easier because with the lack of options, it is easier to decide. That being said, tiny homes discourage separating walls, meaning that there are just that fewer elements to consider while planning your project. To be honest, it is not as easy as it might sound. While yes, there are fewer things to think about, there is a reason that professionals exist in the field. However, if you are going for something simpler, it should be easy enough for you to make your own plans. Being completely honest, this is one of the best parts of making your own tiny home. When looking for your dream house, you can go through dozens of choices before settling for the one that is the closest to your vision. Here, however, your dream becomes your home. You are the boss. You make the choices. You have no reason to settle as you can make whatever adjustments you want.

An eco-friendly life is something that all of us should strive for. With a huge home, we grow further away from this. The amount of cement and similar materials that are used in huge amounts makes your footprint much bigger. Despite your diet of recycling habits, you cannot really say that you are living a green life if you are keeping nature five inches of concrete away. The comfort of huge rooms can be very attractive, I know, and there is nothing wrong with letting it be your primary driving force. However, if all of us went for a greener lifestyle, we would be living in a better world. While it is true that nobody can live completely green. This is impossible even in a tiny house, as you rely on things like electricity and separation from the elements. On the other hand, it is far more eco-friendly than the norm. While you cannot completely delete your footprint, you can make it as small as possible. Tiny homes help you do this by spending as little materials as possible, as well as encouraging you to go for choices that help keep your environment as healthy as possible.

There are flaws in owning a tiny home when compared to a regular size one, of course. If there weren't, everyone would be living in tiny homes. It is very hard to get used to living in one, especially if you lived in huge homes your whole life. There are just so many things that you are going to have to give up on so many things. Is it worth it, though? To be completely honest, there isn't a definite answer to this question. While many people report being the happiest that they have ever been, there have been many that cannot look past the flaws. It is true that the minimalist lifestyle is difficult to accept; it is rewarding beyond limits. Once you throw away everything that isn't necessary for you, you will breathe much more easily. With having fewer things to think about comes more free time. Free time that you can use to pick up many hobbies or dedicate it to other people. However, this balances out. A collection of fancy clothes or your favorite books has a huge chance of being discarded. This can put a dent into your morale. It can be embarrassing to wear the same tuxedo for a few consecutive weddings. It is a very different kind of life, but one that you can get used to. The most difficult period is the one at the beginning. As time goes by, it will become much easier. Once you get acquainted with the lifestyle, and you learn to enjoy it, the short period of time when you had difficulties will disappear from your memories.

Where tiny homes outdo, any other option is the intimacy that you will have with your house. While it is true that after years of living in an apartment or regular-sized house, you will know every bit of your home by heart. It will always feel empty. You will know where everything is, but will it matter if you did not place it there? Building your own home adds a new level of importance to it. Not just the home, but the process as well. While the door frame where you measured and marked your children's growth is a very special place, it becomes so much more special if you were the one who placed it there with this one function in mind. The idyllic feeling of owning your own home, something that you can truly call your own, is just elevated. Any wall that you have placed will feel so much more important because you were the one who placed it there.

It is easy to underestimate the value of love that a person can have for an inanimate object. This is especially true if said object is a key to their life and comfort, as well as happiness. A home is a special place. It is a place where you spend most of the moments of your life, both good and bad. It is a place where you can go back to, no matter what. After the longest of days, the hardest of days, it will be a place of warmth and comfort that can help you get through anything. However, your home might look; it is something that you should love. If you do not, then what is the point? Is living in a place that does not fulfill you worth it?

A tiny home is much easier to love. This might seem like a romantic statement to help advertise tiny homes; it is not. When you build something with your own hands, when you pour your own sweat into it, it becomes so much more important to you. At the end of the day, you will have the singular thought that you built this.

Made in the USA
Las Vegas, NV
08 December 2023

82361344R00066